THE FOOD COMBINING COOK BOOK

A Compendium of Appetizing Recipes that Don't Mix Foods that Fight!

D1119268

THE FOOD COMBINING COOK BOOK
Recipes for the Hay System

by

Erwina Lidolt

Translated by Linda Sonntag
Edited by Lee Faber

Illustrated by Julie Breese

Thorsons
An Imprint of HarperCollins*Publishers*

Thorsons
An Imprint of HarperCollins*Publishers*
77–85 Fulham Palace Road,
Hammersmith, London W6 8JB

First published by Veritas Verlag, Germany as
Voll Wert Trenn Kost, 1983
This fully revised edition published by Thorsons 1987
11 13 15 14 12

© Thorsons Publishing Group 1987

Erwina Lidolt asserts the moral right to
be identified as the author of this work

Illustrated by Julie Breese

A CIP catalogue record for this book
is available from the British Library

ISBN 0-7225-1500-6
ISBN 0-7225-1269-4 Pbk

Printed in Great Britain
by The Bath Press, Bath, Avon

CONTENTS

FOREWORD

The comprehensive selection of health-giving and appetizing recipes in this book should fill a much-felt need for the thousands of people who are following the Hay System since the publication of FOOD COMBINING FOR HEALTH in September, 1984.

We congratulate the author of this book on her delectable and imaginative recipes. They forcefully confirm, moreover, that the Hay System is not a diet in any sense of the word, but a pleasurable and delicious way of eating for health.

DORIS GRANT
AND JEAN JOICE

PREFACE

The Food Combining way of eating was pioneered in 1929 by an American, Dr William Howard Hay, who wrote an influential book called *A New Health Era*.

Dr Hay was suffering from a severe kidney ailment that could not be cured by conventional means, so he experimented with his diet and discovered that his body responded positively when he separated his intake of carbohydrates (starch) and protein, never eating them together in one meal. His theory was based on the premise that the digestion of starch requires alkaline conditions throughout the digestive tract and protein requires acid conditions. By practising his theory, he was able to cure what had been thought of as an incurable disease. He gave him name to this way of eating, which is often called 'The Hay System.'

Since that time it has been shown that food combining works equally well to combat other diseases, such as disorders of the digestive tract, rheumatism and gout. My husband had a severe illness and, on the advice of my doctor, I put him on the Hay System, with the best possible results.

But the Hay System is not only for use in illness. It is for healthy people who believe that prevention is better than cure.

When you are using the Hay System, it is particularly important to avoid refined foods and those containing additives and concentrate on wholefoods and organically-grown produce if possible.

It is with these points in mind that I have compiled this recipe book, which I hope will help many fit people remain healthy and many ill people get better.

Wishing you every success.

ERWINA LIDOLT

9

INTRODUCTION

The Hay System is much more than a diet for those who are sick. It is a natural and delicious way of eating that can also bring a sense of well-being to healthy people and keep them fit and energetic.

It is based on the principle of separating proteins and concentrated carbohydrates, so that they are not eaten together at the same meal. Some meals will be predominantly carbohydrate meals, others predominantly protein meals. Proteins require acid conditions before digestion can take place and carbohydrates need alkaline conditions. It is clear that the stomach cannot provide both at the same time. Because the modern Western diet mixes large quantities of concentrated proteins and starchy processed foods containing readily reabsorbed sugar, our stomachs are obliged to produce an excess of acid; over the years this results, in many cases, in disease.

One of the basic rules of the Hay System is that foods which create alkaline end products in the body — fruit, vegetables and saladings — should form the basis of our daily diet. Bread and other starchy foods, meat, eggs, cheese etc., should form only about a fifth of what we eat. You can increase your energy by eating more carbohydrates, but not by eating more protein. As protein sits more heavily in the stomach than carbohydrates, it is a good idea to eat a protein meal in the middle of the day and a starch meal in the evening. In addition, there is a huge range of neutral foods to choose from; these will go with both protein and starch meals.

If these rules sound a little complicated to the lay ear, a look at the recipes will prove that the Hay System is actually quite easy to follow. Once you have the hang of it, you will also be able to order meals in a restaurant that will fit in with your new way of eating.

At the back of this book (page 120) you will find a table of compatible foods. Looking at this, you can tell at a glance which foods are predominantly starches, which are protein and which are neutral.

I have deliberately not given guidelines for how many servings each recipe makes, as everyone's appetite is different, and people who do heavy manual work will need to eat more than those who sit all day at a desk. However, having said that, most of the recipes will serve 4 people of average appetite.

This book should be a valuable aid to anyone who is nutritionally aware, whether they are well or ill.

General Tips

1. Neutral foods can be eaten at protein or starch meals, but proteins and starches should never be eaten at the same meal.

2. Attempt to eat only one type of protein or starch per meal — fish, meat, eggs or cheese for protein meals and bread, pasta, rice or potatoes for starch meals.

3. Children and those who do heavy manual work can eat two concentrated meals a day (for instance, a protein meal at midday and a starch meal in the evening). People with more sedentary lifestyles should eat only one concentrated meal a day.

4. Use refined or cold-pressed vegetable oils such as sunflower, corn, olive, soya or wheatgerm, which are high in polyunsaturates.

5. Use butter in preference to margarine.

6. When melting butter, do it gently. Do not let it brown.

7. Vegetables should be sweated in their own juices with only a very little water added. Exceptions are cauliflower and asparagus.

8. Instead of frying meat, fish and poultry, cook them gently in a covered pan in their own juices or braise them in the oven.

9. Always pay attention to freshness and quality when shopping for food. Always buy food in season. It will be fresher and cheaper.

10. Eat a small salad of raw vegetables or a piece of fruit before every meal.

11. When preparing salads, try to choose two or more vegetables that have grown below the ground and combine with the same number of vegetables growing above the ground.

12. Avoid all refined and processed foods.

13. Use only honey or fructose (fruit sugar) as sweeteners.

14. Always wait at least four hours after a meal before you eat again.

15. After an afternoon snack, you should not eat any more acidic fruit if your evening meal is starch.

16. Cut down your consumption of salt as much as possible. Use only sea salt.

17. If you do not eat meat, fish, eggs or cheese, choose a potato-based meal in lieu of a protein one.

18. Do not take milk with a meat meal.

19. Soured cream can be used in addition to butter for special occasion dishes.

20. Protein recipes have been designated
    ⒫

    Starch recipes have been designated
    ⒮

    Neutral recipes have been designated
    ⓞ

If a recipe is marked optionally
    ⒮ ⒫
be sure to follow the appropriate instructions for your choice of meal.

Except where stated otherwise, all recipes make four average portions.

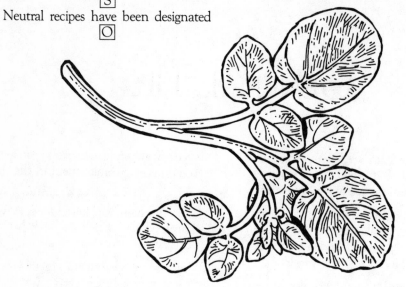

To learn more fully about the Hay System and the principles on which it is based, and thus to obtain maximum benefit from this system of eating, readers are advised to refer to *Food Combining For Health* by Doris Grant and Jean Joice (Thorsons, 1984).

Herbs, Spices and Other Seasonings

Herbs, spices and seasonings are especially important in a wholefood Hay System way of eating. Natural seasonings — leaves, stalks, roots, bulbs, flowers, seeds and bark — offer the cook a huge scope to create an infinite number of different flavours. Seasonings also 'make the mouth water' and stimulate the digestive juices. Each seasoning lends its own particular flavour and medicinal properties: some have a calming effect, others aid the digestion, relieve cramp or act as stimulants. Care should be taken when combining seasonings, as they don't all go together well. It is better to err by using too little, rather than too much — you can always add a little more.

If possible, always use fresh herbs. Freshly picked from the garden, they have a strong, true aroma and taste and they are far more beneficial to the health than dried or powdered herbs, which quickly lose their strength. If you don't have a garden, herbs can be grown quite easily in a window box or in pots on the window sill.

To dry fresh herbs for the winter months, hang them up away from direct sunlight, then store in dark glass screw-topped jars in a cool place. Some herbs can also be successfully frozen. Wash them, then dry on absorbent kitchen paper. Chop finely and freeze individually in small containers or in an ice cube tray. (Celery leaves can also be preserved in this manner, for use in soups or as a garnish.)

If you can identify herbs, take a paper bag along when you go out walking in the countryside. You will find plenty of wild plants to collect and take home, e.g., sorrel and dandelion in the spring and wild thyme in the autumn.

Salt should always be used very sparingly. Too much salt can cause hardening of the arteries and contribute to high blood-pressure and other ailments. The body does not require more than one or two grams of salt a day, yet on the average, we consume a horrifying 10-20g!

If you must use salt, sea salt is the best type, as it does not absorb as much water, but you can compensate for the lack of salt by using other seasonings, such as celery, garlic, onion and lemon balm, for instance, in more generous quantities.

Herbs

BASIL can be used in most savoury dishes and is especially good in those that contain tomatoes. It is also an important ingredient in Italian cuisine. Try it in soups, sauces and dressings, stuffings, herb butter and casseroles.

BAY LEAVES are tied into bouquets garnis. They can also be used on their own, either whole or crumbled to flavour sauces, soups, vegetables and stews. Always discard whole bay leaves before serving.

BORAGE has a delicate, cucumber-like flavour. Young leaves can be added to salads, spinach and quark. It can be used in generous quantities as it is quite mild. (The flowers are edible also.)

CELERY. The leaves can be used as an herb in salads, vegetable and potato soup and savoury spreads.

CHERVIL is a relative of parsley, with a hint of a liquorice flavour. Large amounts can be used in fish dishes, herb butters and vegetables, especially carrots. It also brings out the flavour of other herbs and is used in fines herbes mixtures.

CHIVES are the most delicate member of the onion family. They can be added to salads and herb butters, sprinkled over soups and incorporated into soured cream dressings. Do not cook them.

DILLWEED is an excellent addition to fish, especially salmon. It can also be used with vegetables, soups, sauces, potatoes and cucumber salads.

FENNEL. Herb fennel, with its feathery leaves, has a fresh flavour reminiscent of liquorice and is very good with white fish. It is also good in green and potato salads, sauces and vegetables.

LEMON BALM has a distinct lemon flavour. It is slightly bitter, so should be used sparingly. It can be added to vegetables, meat, fish, poultry, sauces, salads, marinades and cream cheese mixtures.

LOVAGE is both a culinary and medicinal herb. The strong celery-like flavour enhances soups, casseroles, sauces, vegetables, salads, meat and rice dishes.

MARJORAM also called 'sweet marjoram', has a spicy, faintly sweet flavour. It is used in soups, stews, sauces, vegetables and salads and has an affinity with poultry.

MINT. There are many varieties of mint, each with its own distinctive flavour. It is often used as an accompaniment to lamb and is very nice with fresh peas, fruit and vegetable salads.

OREGANO is also known as 'wild marjoram'. It is quite pungent and can be successfully used in pasta and pizza and other Italian dishes. It is also a good addition to vegetable dishes, especially those containing tomatoes, aubergines, courgettes and peppers. It is usually used dried.

PARSLEY is a good accompaniment to almost any dish. It can also be used as a garnish and makes a lovely sauce. Do not always cook parsley, but add it to the finished dish for a nice, crunchy texture.

ROSEMARY has a pungent, distinctive flavour which may overpower other herbs, so it is best used on its own with lamb, poultry, root vegetables and fish.

SAGE is a favourite Italian flavouring. It can also be used in cheese spreads, casseroles, stews and sauces.

SAVORY. Both winter and summer savory have a peppery flavour, but the summer variety is particularly good with runner and broad beans. Both can be used in cucumber and potato salads, beef casseroles, cheese dishes and tomato sauces. It is also an interesting addition to savoury baking.

SORREL is a very versatile herb. It can be used raw in salads, cooked as a vegetable and a delicate flavouring for soup.

TARRAGON is often used with chicken. It also combines well with cream sauces, vinegars and herb purées.

THYME can be used in soups, stuffings, casseroles and sauces. It goes well with most meats and is a nice addition to poaching liquid for fish and salad dressings.

WATERCRESS is not strictly a herb, but can be used as one. It is also good in salads and as a garnish. It can be found growing wild in the springtime on the banks of streams.

Note: If you are substituting dried herbs for the fresh herbs used in the following recipes, use only one-quarter to half the quantity specified.

SPICES AND OTHER SEASONINGS

ALLSPICE can be added to both sweet and savoury dishes. It can be bought whole or ground; it is not a combination of spices, but tastes like cloves, cinnamon and nutmeg. It is a good addition to red cabbage and fruit compotes.

ANISEED can be used whole or ground for both savoury and sweet dishes. It is often used in baking, fruit salads and with vegetables such as carrots, pumpkin and red cabbage.

CAPERS can be used with meat or fish and in sauces, marinades and spreads.

CARDAMOM has a light, sweetish-spicy flavour that enhances baked goods and hot drinks. It is a popular ingredient of Indian cuisine and can be used with meat, poultry and rice.

CHILLI PEPPERS are very hot, so should be used sparingly. The seeds are the hottest part, so if you prefer milder flavours, discard them. Always wash your hands well after handling chillies. Use in minced meat, stews and sauces.

CINNAMON can be bought in sticks or ground. The sticks will infuse flavour into hot drinks and fruit compotes, while ground cinnamon is compatible with rice pudding, fruit compotes, apples and fruit cakes.

CLOVES are used both whole and ground. Whole cloves are added to marinades and are used stuck in onions for infusing hotpots and sauces. Ground cloves are used as a flavouring in baking, and fruit compotes.

CORIANDER SEEDS have a fresh, spicy flavour and are used in many Indian dishes. They also enhance cabbage and carrots. Do not buy ground coriander. It loses its aroma very quickly, but you can grind it yourself to use in bread and other baked goods.

CUMIN SEEDS are also frequently used in Indian and Middle Eastern cookery. The whole seeds are also used for pickling.

CURRY POWDER. Commercial curry powder is a combination of many spices. It is best to make your own. It is used, of course, for vegetable, meat and poultry curries and rice dishes. If you do buy a commercial blend, you can choose from a mild or hot mixture.

GARLIC is the strongest member of the onion family. It will enhance most savoury dishes. Use it generously with vegetables, salads and dressings, meat and poultry and sauces. It is reputed to be very healthy.

JUNIPER BERRIES are always bought whole, but can be easily ground. They are often used in meat and game marinades and can also be added to casseroles, beetroot and cabbage.

MACE is the outer part of nutmeg. It is available in blade form and ground. The flavour is similar to nutmeg, but milder. Use for soups and stews, cheese sauces and cakes.

MUSTARD AND CRESS is generally used as a garnish and in salads. It is not as strongly flavoured as watercress.

19

NUTMEG should be bought whole and freshly grated. Use it sparingly in cream sauces, with spinach, in hot drinks, soups, cakes and biscuits.

ONION is also reputed to be beneficial to health. Use it often in all savoury dishes.

PAPRIKA is sold ground and is an essential ingredient in goulash. It is also an attractive garnish for pale-coloured savoury dishes and fish. Hungarian paprika is the sweetest.

PEPPER is available whole and ground, but it is better to buy whole peppercorns and grind them yourself. Black pepper is used in most savoury dishes, but it also has an astonishing affinity with some fruits, especially strawberries. Green peppercorns are usually sold pickled in brine. White pepper is milder than black and is used in delicately flavoured dishes and white sauces.

POPPY SEEDS are derived from the opium poppy and have a nutty flavour. They are often sprinkled on bread and rolls and used as a filling for sweet pastries.

SESAME SEEDS have a nutty flavour. They can be toasted and used in salads, or sprinkled over bread, poultry and vegetables. Sesame oil is derived from the seeds.

VANILLA PODS are used to flavour sweet dishes and drinks. The pods can be re-used if they are dried well and stored in a screw-topped glass jar.

SPROUTING GRAINS AND SEEDS

Sprouting grains and seeds at home is very easy to do. You can buy special sprouting equipment from health food shops, but sprouting is just as easy to accomplish in a jam jar or a soup plate.

Sprouts offer a valuable supplement to your diet, especially in the winter months when home-grown salad vegetables are unavailable.

All kinds of grain are suitable for sprouting, as well as soya beans, chickpeas, lentils, sunflower seeds, mustard seeds, fenugreek and alfalfa.

Sprouted grains can be used in stuffings for vegetables and poultry or in soups and salads.

Sprouted seeds are especially good in salads or used as a garnish for other foods. The kernels of sprouted mustard seeds should be used very sparingly, as they are very sharp-flavoured.

Seeds will sprout and be ready to be harvested in 2-6 days, according to type. Do not sprout too large a batch at once — a small amount, harvested often, will provide you with a constant supply of fresh food.

Do not discard the water used to rinse your seeds. It contains useful nutrients which can be used to water your house plants.

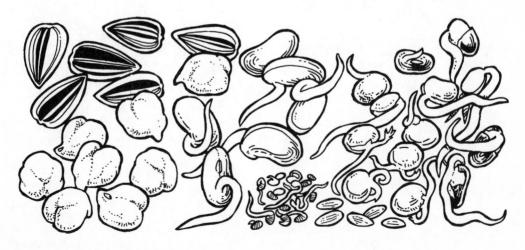

SALADS

I have paid special attention to this chapter since salads and raw vegetables play such an important role in the Hay System. Salads contain fibre, which is essential for the digestion, as well as many valuable vitamins.

Vegetable and fruit salads should be eaten as a prelude to meals for the best effect on the stomach and digestive tract. The more substantial meat, fish and pasta salads should be served as main meals.

Salads for starch meals can be tossed in a cream dressing. Use lemon juice or cider vinegar on salads to be served with protein meals. Vinaigrette dressings and flavoured oils can be stored in tightly sealed jars in the refrigerator; add chopped onion and garlic, green peppercorns, a few basil leaves and a sprig of rosemary or thyme. This way, you will always have the basis for a delicious salad dressing to hand. Add seasoning to taste and shake the jar well before use.

Brewer's yeast is an important source of Vitamin B and is a valuable addition to salad dressing. One teaspoonful is sufficient for 4 people.

RAW ASPARAGUS SALAD ○

1 lb (450g) very young asparagus
¼ pint (140ml) soured cream
1 teaspoonful mustard powder
1 tablespoonful finely chopped
parsley
Young salad leaves

1. Peel the asparagus and trim off any woody bits. (If the asparagus is really young, it is not necessary to do this.) Cut into 2-inch (5cm) lengths and set aside.

2. Make the dressing. Mix the soured cream, mustard powder and parsley together well. Toss lightly with the asparagus.

3. Place a bed of salad leaves on individual plates and arrange the asparagus on top.

GREEN BEAN SALAD ℗

1 lb (450g) runner beans
1 onion, sliced
1 green pepper, deseeded and cut
into julienne strips
1 red pepper, deseeded and cut into
julienne strips
1 yellow pepper, deseeded and cut
into julienne strips
2 cloves garlic, crushed
1½ tablespoonsful cold-pressed olive
oil
1½ tablespoonsful cider vinegar
Few drops soy sauce
Pinch of mustard powder
Pinch of chopped savory

1. Cut the beans into 1-inch (2.5cm) lengths.

2. Place the beans in a covered medium-sized saucepan with a few tablespoonsful of water and cook over moderate heat for 2 minutes. Remove from the heat, drain and set aside to cool.

3. Place the onion, green, red and yellow peppers and garlic in a salad bowl.

4. Make the dressing. Place the oil, vinegar, soy sauce, mustard powder and savory in a screw-topped jar and shake to combine. Pour over the ingredients in the salad bowl, add the beans and toss well.

COOKED BEETROOT SALAD [P]

1 lb (450g) beetroot, cooked and peeled
2 tablespoonsful cold-pressed olive oil
1½ tablespoonsful cider vinegar
1 teaspoonful cumin seeds
Sea salt and freshly ground black pepper to taste

1. Slice the beetroot into a salad bowl.

2. Make the dressing. Mix together the oil, vinegar, cumin, salt and pepper and pour over the beetroot. Mix gently and leave to marinate for at least an hour before serving.

RAW BEETROOT SALAD [P]

1 lb (450g) raw beetroot, peeled
2 tablespoonsful cold-pressed olive oil
1½ tablespoonsful cider vinegar
1 teaspoonful cumin seeds
Sea salt and freshly ground black pepper to taste

1. Grate the beetroot finely into a salad bowl.

2. Make the dressing. Mix together the oil, vinegar, cumin, salt and pepper and pour over the beetroot. Mix well and leave to marinate for at least an hour before serving.

Belgian Endive [S][P] Salad

2 Belgian endives
1½-2 tablespoonsful cold-pressed
olive oil
1½ tablespoonsful cider vinegar
Sea salt and freshly ground black
pepper to taste

1. Wash and drain the endive, then cut into shreds. Place in a salad bowl.

2. Make the dressing. Place the oil, vinegar, salt, pepper and onion in a screw-topped jar and shake to combine. Pour the dressing over the endive and serve, as a **protein** salad.

Variations:

1. Replace salad dressing with Yogurt Sauce (page 97). Toss with the endives for a **protein** meal.

2. Toss the endives with seasoned soured cream for a **starch** meal.

3. Substitute soured cream for the yogurt in Yogurt Sauce (page 97). Add sliced boiled potatoes and serve with a starch meal.

Raw Cabbage [P] Salad

1 lb (450g) white cabbage
¼ pint (140ml) sunflower oil
3 fl oz (90ml) cider vinegar
Sea salt and freshly ground black
pepper to taste
1 teaspoonful cumin seeds

1. Coarsely grate or finely chop the cabbage into a salad bowl.

2. Place the remaining ingredients in a screw-topped jar and shake to combine. Pour over the cabbage and mix well.

3. Marinate the salad in the refrigerator for at least 1 hour before serving.

Red Cabbage [P] Slaw

1 lb (450g) red cabbage
1 red apple, unpeeled
¼ pint (140ml) soured cream
1 tablespoonful lemon juice
Sea salt to taste
1 tablespoonful finely chopped
onion

1. Chop the cabbage finely and place in a salad bowl. Core the apple and grate into the bowl with the cabbage.

2. Make the dressing by mixing the remaining ingredients together. Pour over the cabbage and mix well to combine. Leave to marinate for 1 hour before serving.

CARROT SALAD $\boxed{S}\boxed{P}$

1 lb (450g) carrots, scraped
¼ pint (140ml) vinaigrette dressing
(page 97) *or*
¼ pint (140ml) soured cream
Sea salt and freshly ground black
pepper to taste

1. Grate the carrots into a salad bowl.

2. Toss with vinaigrette dressing for a **protein** meal or soured cream for a **starch** meal. Season to taste.

CARROT AND CELERY SALAD $\boxed{S}\boxed{P}$

3 fl oz (90ml) sunflower oil and
2 fl oz (60ml) lemon juice *or*
¼ pint (150ml) soured cream and
1 tablespoonful finely chopped fresh
herbs
½ lb (225g) carrots, scraped
½ lb (225g) celery
Sea salt and freshly ground black
pepper to taste
1 tablespoonful finely chopped
hazelnuts

1. First make the dressing using the oil and lemon juice for a **protein** meal or the soured cream and herbs for a **starch** meal. Pour into a salad bowl.

2. Grate the carrots and celery into the dressing and stir immediately to prevent the vegetables from discolouring.

3. Allow the salad to marinate for at least 30 minutes, then sprinkle with hazelnuts and serve.

RAW CAULIFLOWER SALAD $\boxed{P}$

1 cauliflower, separated into very
small florets
2 tablespoonsful finely chopped
parsley
2 tablespoonsful finely chopped
onion
2 tomatoes, skinned and chopped
(optional)
3 fl oz (90ml) sunflower oil
2 fl oz (60ml) cider vinegar
Sea salt and freshly ground black
pepper to taste

1. Place the cauliflower florets (reserve the core for a vegetable soup), parsley, onion and tomatoes, if using, in a salad bowl.

2. Combine the oil, vinegar and seasoning and pour over the salad. Toss well and allow to marinate for at least 30 minutes before serving.

COOKED CELERIAC SALAD ⬚S ⬚P

1 celeriac root, cooked
2 tablespoonsful cold-pressed olive oil and
1½ tablespoonsful cider vinegar *or*
4 tablespoonsful soured cream
Sea salt and freshly ground black pepper
1 tablespoonful chopped onion

1. Peel the celeriac and cut into julienne strips. Place in a salad bowl.

2. Make the dressing. Mix together the oil and vinegar (**protein** meal) or soured cream (**starch** meal) with the salt, pepper and onion. Pour over the celeriac and toss well to combine.

RAW CELERIAC SALAD ⬚S ⬚P

2 tablespoonsful cold-pressed olive oil and
1½ tablespoonsful cider vinegar *or*
4 tablespoonsful soured cream
Sea salt and freshly ground black pepper
1 celeriac root
Chopped chives and celeriac leaves to garnish

1. First make the dressing by mixing together the oil and vinegar (**protein** meal) or soured cream (**starch** meal) with the salt and pepper in a salad bowl.

2. Grate the celeriac into the salad bowl and stir immediately to prevent discolouration.

3. Sprinkle with chopped chives and celeriac leaves.

CHINESE LEAVES ⬚P

1 head Chinese leaves
1½-2 tablespoonsful cold-pressed olive oil
1½ tablespoonsful cider vinegar
Sea salt and freshly ground black pepper to taste
1 clove garlic, crushed
Thinly sliced leeks, onions *or* cucumber to garnish

1. Shred the Chinese leaves or cut them into thin strips.

2. Make the dressing. Place the oil, vinegar, salt, pepper and garlic in a screw-topped jar and shake to combine. Toss Chinese leaves with dressing and place in a salad bowl.

3. Garnish with leeks, onions or cucumber.

COURGETTE SALAD ⬚P

1 lb (450g) young courgettes
Sea salt
1 clove garlic, finely chopped
1 teaspoonful chopped lemon balm
1 teaspoonful chopped dillweed
3 tablespoonsful sunflower oil
1½ tablespoonsful cider vinegar

1. Slice the courgettes very finely, sprinkle with salt and leave to sweat for 30 minutes. Rinse and pat dry with absorbent kitchen paper.

2. Place courgettes in a salad bowl and sprinkle with garlic, lemon balm and dillweed.

3. Combine the oil and vinegar and pour over the salad. Toss well.

CUCUMBER SALAD S P

1½-2 tablespoonsful cold-pressed
olive oil and
1½ tablespoonsful cider vinegar or
3 tablespoonsful soured cream
Sea salt and freshly ground black
pepper to taste
1 clove garlic, crushed
Pinch of chopped borage
1 cucumber, thinly sliced
Pinch of finely chopped dillweed

1. First make the dressing. Combine the
oil and vinegar (**protein** meal) or soured
cream (**starch** meal) with the salt, garlic
and borage.

2. Combine the dressing and cucumber
in a salad bowl and sprinkle with
dillweed.

CUCUMBER-CORN SALAD S

1 cucumber, diced
2 shallots, finely chopped
½ lb (225g) fresh or frozen
sweetcorn, cooked
2 fl oz (60ml) corn oil
Sea salt and freshly ground black
pepper to taste
1 clove garlic, crushed
Chopped dillweed and chives to
garnish

1. Mix together the cucumber, shallots
and sweetcorn in a salad bowl.

2. Make the dressing. Mix together the
oil, salt, pepper and garlic. Pour over the
salad and mix well.

3. Garnish with chopped dillweed and
chives.

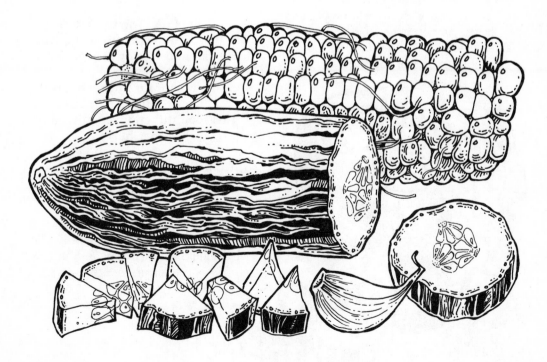

PIQUANT FARMHOUSE SALAD   P

1 red pepper, deseeded and cut into
rings
1 onion, sliced
2 courgettes, sliced
2 tomatoes, sliced
½ cucumber, sliced
4 black olives, stoned and chopped
1 oz (30g) goat's cheese, cubed
3 tablespoonsful cold-pressed
olive oil
2 tablespoonsful cider vinegar
Sea salt and freshly ground black
pepper to taste
1 teaspoonful chopped herbs

1. Place the red pepper, onion,
courgettes, tomatoes, cucumber, olives
and cheese in a salad bowl.

2. Make the dressing. Mix together the
oil and vinegar with the salt, pepper and
herbs. Pour over the salad and mix
carefully, taking care not to break up the
cubes of cheese.

FENNEL SALAD WITH SOURED CREAM   P

1 fennel bulb, finely chopped
2 stalks celery, finely chopped
1 apple, coarsely grated
3 tablespoonsful soured cream
Sea salt and freshly ground black
pepper to taste
1 large clove garlic, crushed

1. Combine the fennel, celery and apple
in a salad bowl.

2. Mix the soured cream with the salt,
pepper and garlic.

3. Toss the salad with the dressing and
allow to marinate for 15 minutes before
serving.

POTATO SALAD   S

1 lb (450g) waxy potatoes
2½ fl oz (75ml) cold-pressed olive oil
Sea salt and freshly ground black
pepper
1 tablespoonful finely chopped
onion
1 teaspoonful chopped chervil *or*
other herbs

1. Cook the potatoes in their skins until
tender, drain and allow to cool, then peel
and slice.

2. Place the potatoes in a salad bowl and
mix with the remaining ingredients. This
salad should be eaten very fresh or it will
be difficult to digest.

FRENCH POTATO SALAD [S]

1 lb (450g) waxy potatoes, unpeeled
1 medium-sized carrot, diced
1 kohlrabi bulb, diced
1 stalk celery, chopped
2 oz (55g) cauliflower florets, chopped
2 oz (55g) peas
Home-made Mayonnaise (page 94)
Lettuce leaves and chopped chives to serve

1. Cook the potatoes in their skins until tender, drain and allow to cool. Cut into large dice and place in a salad bowl.

2. Cook the remaining vegetables until just tender and add to the potatoes.

3. Moisten the salad with a few tablespoonsful mayonnaise, then toss lightly to coat.

4. Set the salad aside for 30 minutes to allow the flavours to mingle, then serve on individual salad plates on a bed of lettuce. Sprinkle with chives.

Note: The recipe on page 94 for mayonnaise should be used in this recipe, since traditional or shop-bought mayonnaise is incompatible with a starch meal.

RADICCHIO SALAD [O]

1-2 heads radicchio
1 onion, finely chopped
3 fl oz (90ml) cold-pressed olive oil
1 tablespoonful mustard powder
Sea salt to taste
Chopped chives to garnish

1. Wash the radicchio and tear into bite-sized pieces. Place in a salad bowl with the onion.

2. Mix together the oil, mustard powder and salt and pour over the salad. Toss to combine.

3. Garnish with chopped chives.

RADISH AND KOHLRABI SALAD [S] [P]

1 small bunch radishes, stalks removed
2 medium-sized kohlrabi bulbs
1½-2 tablespoonsful cold-pressed olive oil and
1½ tablespoonsful cider vinegar *or*
3 tablespoonsful soured cream
Sea salt to taste
1 tablespoonful finely chopped dillweed
Young salad leaves

1. Grate together the radishes and kohlrabi into a salad bowl.

2. Make the dressing. Mix together the oil and vinegar (**protein** meal) or soured cream (**starch** meal) with the salt and dillweed. Mix into the radishes and kohlrabi.

3. To serve, place a bed of young salad leaves on individual plates and top with a mound of salad.

ROOT VEGETABLE SALAD [P]

½ lb (225g) turnips
1 celeriac root
½ lb (225g) carrots
1½-2 tablespoonsful cold-pressed
olive oil
1½ tablespoonsful cider vinegar
1 teaspoonful mustard powder
Few drops soy sauce
Sea salt to taste
Lettuce leaves to serve
Finely chopped onion and fresh
herbs

1. Finely grate the turnips, celeriac and carrots, keeping the vegetables separate.

2. Make the dressing. Place the oil, vinegar, mustard powder, soy sauce and salt in a screw-topped jar and shake to combine. Toss each vegetable with dressing.

3. Line individual salad plates with lettuce leaves and place a mound of each grated vegetable on top.

4. Sprinkle with chopped onion and herbs.

SPINACH SALAD [P]

½ lb (225g) young spinach leaves,
tough stalks removed
1 tart apple, cored and diced
3 firm tomatoes, diced
¼ cucumber, diced
½ bunch watercress, tough stalks
removed
4 hard-boiled eggs
3 tablespoonsful sunflower oil
1 tablespoonful cider vinegar
1 clove garlic, crushed
Sea salt and freshly ground black
pepper to taste
Radish slices to garnish

1. Wash spinach, drain well and tear into manageable pieces. Place in a salad bowl. Add the apple, tomatoes, cucumber and watercress.

2. Shell the eggs, chop and add to the mixture in the salad bowl.

3. Make the dressing. Mix together the oil, vinegar, garlic, salt and pepper and pour over the salad. Mix carefully to prevent breaking up the eggs.

4. Garnish with sliced radish.

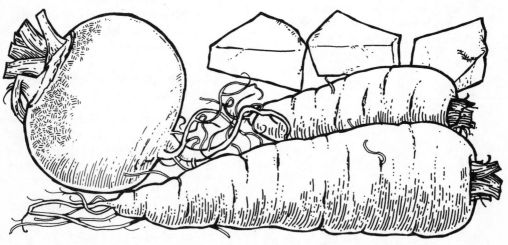

TOMATO AND PEPPER SALAD [P]

1 green pepper, deseeded
1 red pepper, deseeded
1 yellow pepper, deseeded
4 tomatoes, sliced
2 tablespoonsful finely chopped
onion
1 clove garlic, crushed
3 tablespoonsful cold-pressed olive
oil
2 tablespoonsful cider vinegar
Sea salt and freshly ground black
pepper to taste
1 oz (30g) goat's cheese (optional)

1. Finely chop the green, red and yellow peppers into a salad bowl. Add the tomatoes and onion.

2. Make the dressing. Place the garlic, oil, vinegar, salt and pepper in a screw-topped jar and shake to combine. Pour over the salad and toss lightly.

3. Crumble the goat's cheese over the salad and serve.

CHEESE SALAD [P]

½ lb (225g) Emmental cheese
2 oz (55g) radishes, grated
2 oz (55g) carrots, grated
1 recipe quantity Yogurt Sauce
(page 97)
Chopped parsley, chervil, watercress
or sorrel to garnish

1. Grate the cheese coarsely and place in a salad bowl with the radishes and carrots.

2. Toss the salad with the dressing and marinate in the refrigerator for 30 minutes.

3. Just before serving, sprinkle with parsley, chervil, watercress or sorrel.

CHEESE AND FRUIT SALAD [P]

½ lb (225g) Emmental or Gruyère
cheese, cut into julienne strips
1 slice fresh pineapple, chopped
1 ripe fresh peach, chopped
1 kiwi fruit, chopped
¼ pint (140ml) natural yogurt
1 teaspoonful curry powder
A few green peppercorns, crushed
2 teaspoonsful walnut oil
Pinch of grated nutmeg
Sea salt to taste
Juice of ½ lemon

1. Place the cheese, pineapple, peach and kiwi fruit in a salad bowl.

2. Make the dressing by combining the remaining ingredients. Toss with the cheese and fruit and chill in the refrigerator until needed.

CHICKEN SALAD [P]

1½ lb (680g) cooked chicken, diced
½ lb (225g) celery, diced
1 tart apple, chopped
2 oranges, peeled, deseeded and chopped
Handful of chopped walnuts
2 tablespoonsful finely chopped onion, sorrel or chervil
¼ pint (140ml) mayonnaise
1 tablespoonful lemon juice

1. Mix together all the ingredients except the mayonnaise and lemon juice in a salad bowl.

2. Combine the mayonnaise and lemon juice, add to the salad and mix well.

3. Chill in the refrigerator for at least 1 hour. Serve chilled.

CHICKEN-STUFFED TOMATOES [P]

4 large ripe tomatoes
4 oz (115g) cooked chicken, diced
2 oz (55g) walnuts, chopped
1 very tart apple, peeled, cored and grated
1 tablespoonful lemon juice
Sea salt and freshly ground black pepper
Pinch of paprika
1 teaspoonful finely chopped chervil
6 tablespoonsful mayonnaise

1. Place the tomatoes in boiling water for 1 minute, then drain, skin, carefully cut off the tops and scoop out the flesh. Reserve flesh and place tomato shells upside down to drain.

2. Mix together the reserved tomato flesh with the remaining ingredients. Fill the tomatoes with this mixture and replace the lids.

HERRING SALAD [P]

½ lb (225g) fresh broad beans
½ lb (225g) French beans, cut into 1-inch (2.5cm) lengths
1 onion, chopped
1 green pepper, deseeded and chopped
1 red pepper, deseeded and chopped
2 tomatoes, skinned and chopped
2 rollmop herrings, cut into manageable pieces
2 hard-boiled eggs, sliced
Vinaigrette dressing (page 97) flavoured with fresh thyme and basil
Mustard and cress to garnish

1. Place the broad beans in a medium-sized saucepan with a few tablespoonsful of lightly salted water. Cook over moderate heat until almost tender, then add the French beans and cook briefly. Drain and allow to cool.

2. Place the cooled beans in a salad bowl with the onion, peppers, tomatoes, herrings and eggs. Add a few tablespoonsful vinaigrette dressing and mix lightly. Garnish with mustard and cress.

PASTA SALAD [S]

1 lb (450g) wholewheat pasta shapes
1 stalk celery, diced
1 carrot, scraped and diced
1 ripe pear, cored and chopped
1 gherkin, chopped
2 oz (55g) fresh or frozen peas,
cooked
1 recipe quantity Home-made
Mayonnaise (page 94)
2 tablespoonsful soured cream
Sea salt and freshly ground black
pepper
Chopped basil, chervil *or* chives to
garnish

1. Cook the pasta in plenty of salted water until *al dente*. Drain and refresh under cold water. Set aside.

2. Place the pasta in a salad bowl and add the celery, carrot, pear, gherkin and peas.

3. Mix the mayonnaise with the soured cream and season to taste. Pour the dressing over the salad, mix well and marinate for a couple of hours. Chill if desired.

4. Just before serving, sprinkle with basil, chervil or chives.

Note: The recipe on page 94 for mayonnaise should be used in this recipe, since traditional or shop-bought mayonnaise is incompatible with a starch meal.

PASTA AND VEGETABLE SALAD [S]

1 lb (450g) wholewheat pasta shapes
4 carrots, scraped and diced
4 oz (115g) button mushrooms, sliced
4 oz (115g) very young fresh peas *or*
frozen petits pois, cooked
¼ pint (140ml) Home-made
Mayonnaise (page 94)
¼ pint (140ml) soured cream
Generous handful of chopped fresh
herbs

1. Cook the pasta in plenty of lightly salted water until *al dente*. Drain and refresh under cold water. Set aside.

2. Mix the vegetables with the mayonnaise and soured cream in a serving bowl. Add the herbs and pasta and serve at room temperature or chill in the refrigerator until needed.

Variations:
The mayonnaise may be blended with cream cheese instead of soured cream. In the summer, add diced tomatoes or green and red peppers and serve the salad on a bed of lettuce leaves.

Note: The recipe on page 94 for mayonnaise should be used in this recipe, since traditional or shop-bought mayonnaise is incompatible with a starch meal.

SOUPS

Soup should not be served at the beginning of a meal, as is the normal custom. It is much healthier to start a meal with a salad. Soups should be 'almost-main meals'. They are easily digested and do not lie heavily on the stomach, which makes them particularly suitable for evening meals.

Vegetable soups offer such a huge variety to the cook that you never need to serve the same one twice. All vegetables in season can be used to make both clear and thick soups. Vary the herbs you use to increase your repertoire even further.

If you are tempted to use a vegetable stock cube, read the label on the packet carefully. Most of the commercial brands contain starch, salt, flavour enhancers and preservatives. There are a few truly natural vegetable stocks sold. Your best bet is to check the health food shops.

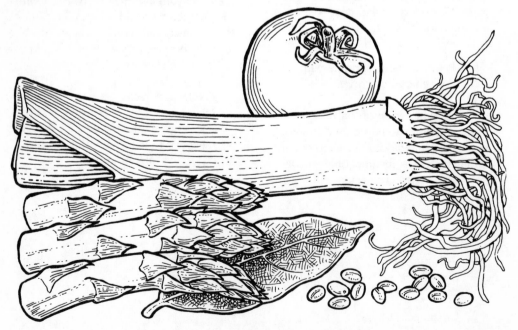

VEGETABLE STOCK (BASIC RECIPE) ⟨O⟩

Slice an onion and sauté with some crushed garlic in a little butter. Meanwhile, cut up any leftover vegetables or bits you have discarded, like the woody ends of asparagus, pea pods, bean pods, outer leaves from a cabbage, carrot peel, the green part of leeks, celery leaves, cauliflower stalks etc. Add these to the pan with some lovage and a chopped Hamburg parsley root, if obtainable, cover with water and simmer for about 20 minutes (better yet, cook in a pressure cooker for 10 minutes) and strain through a sieve. This vegetable stock can be successfully frozen in small batches.

SUPPLEMENTS AND GARNISHES FOR CLEAR SOUPS

STRACCIATELLA ⟨S⟩⟨P⟩

Whisk 1 egg yolk with a little still mineral water, sea salt and wholemeal flour until thick and smooth (**starch**), add it gradually to the cooking soup and continue to cook for a couple of minutes until it has set in the 'little rags' that give the soup its name in Italian. Serve sprinkled with herbs. For a **protein** meal, use a whole egg and soya flour.

SHREDDED OMELETTE ⟨S⟩⟨P⟩

Beat 1 egg with 2 teaspoonful cream and a little soya flour (**protein**) or beat the yolk with wholemeal flour (**starch**), add sea salt to taste and a pinch of nutmeg or marjoram. Heat a little butter in an omelette pan, pour in the egg and let it cook slowly until set. Allow the omelette to cool, cut into strips and add to the hot soup. Omelette made with soya flour can also form an acompaniment to a **protein** meal.

OATFLAKE DUMPLINGS ⟨S⟩

Mix together 1 egg yolk, 2 teaspoonful butter, a little seat salt and some chopped parsley. Stir in 4 teaspoonful oatflakes. Add tiny spoonsful of the mixture to the cooking soup and continue to cook until they are done. Garnish with chopped chives.

NOODLE SOUP ⟨S⟩

Cook some wholewheat noodles or spinach noodles until *al dente*, add to the hot soup and garnish with chopped chives.

RICE SOUP ⟨S⟩

Make this when you have some brown rice (or brown rice and vegetables) left over from another meal. Add to the cooking soup, heat through and serve with chopped herbs.

THICK SOUPS

CREAM OF ASPARAGUS SOUP ☐O

1 lb (450g) asparagus (see note below)
1¾ pints (1 litre) lightly salted water
½ oz (15g) butter
½ tablespoonful potato flour
Pinch of grated nutmeg
Few asparagus tips (optional)
1 hard-boiled egg yolk, chopped, to garnish
Chopped chives and parsley to garnish

1. Wash the asparagus, peel if necessary, cut into short lengths and cook in the lightly salted water until soft, about 30-40 minutes. Remove from the heat.

2. Strain off the asparagus water, reserving it. Purée the asparagus in a blender.

3. Melt the butter in a medium-sized saucepan over moderate heat, add the flour and cook for 1 minute. Add the reserved asparagus water and asparagus purée. Cook until hot, then remove from the heat.

4. Season with nutmeg and add the asparagus tips, if using. Garnish with chopped egg yolk, chives and parsley.

Note: For this soup, you can either use a cheaper variety of asparagus or, if you want to use the tips for another dish, use only the less tender stalks.

BARLEY SOUP ☐S

1½ oz (40g) barley, finely ground
½ pint (300ml) Vegetable Stock (page 37)
½ teaspoon ground cumin seeds
½ teaspoon fennel seeds
Pinch of sea salt

1. Stir the barley into the vegetable stock in a small saucepan. Cook gently over moderate heat for about 10 minutes. Remove from the heat and season with cumin, fennel and salt.

2. Allow the soup to stand for 15 minutes to give the barley time to swell, then warm through again. Eat it slowly!

Note: This soup is very good for an upset stomach and should be eaten several days in a row. If you do not have stomach problems, add a knob of butter and sprinkle with chopped herbs.

ITALIAN CARROT SOUP ☐O

½ lb (225g) carrots, scraped and diced
Few tablespoonsful water
Pinch of sea salt
1 teaspoonful potato flour
1¾ pints (1 litre) Vegetable Stock (page 37)
1 egg yolk
2 tablespoonsful soured cream
Chopped dillweed to garnish

1. Place the carrots and water in a medium-sized saucepan over moderate heat and cook, covered for 1-2 minutes. Add salt and flour, and cook for 1 minute, stirring constantly. Pour over the

vegetable stock and cook gently until the carrots are soft. Remove from the heat.

2. Break the egg yolk into a soup tureen, stir in the soured cream and pour the soup over, stirring constantly. Serve immediately, sprinkled with chopped dillweed.

CAULIFLOWER SOUP [S]

1 large cauliflower
¾ oz (20g) butter
1 teaspoonful potato flour
1¾ pints (1 litre) Vegetable Stock
(page 37)
1 egg yolk
1 tablespoonful soured cream
Chopped fresh herbs to garnish

1. Separate the cauliflower into small florets, chop the stalk and cover with lightly salted water. Set aside for 30 minutes, then drain.

2. Cook the cauliflower in a small amount of fresh, lightly salted water until soft. Do not drain. You can either purée just the stalk and leave the florets whole or purée all the cauliflower at this point for an excellent creamy texture.

3. Melt the butter in a medium-sized saucepan over moderate heat. Stir in the flour and cook for 1 minute. Pour over the vegetable stock and heat until soup thickens. Add the cauliflower and heat through, then remove from the heat.

4. Stir the egg yolk and soured cream into the soup and garnish with chopped herbs.

CREAM CHEESE-HERB SOUP [S]

¾ oz (20g) butter
4 teaspoonsful wholemeal flour
1¾ pints (1 litre) Vegetable Stock
(page 37)
2 tablespoonsful cream cheese
Pinch of grated nutmeg
Sea salt to taste
2 tablespoonsful soured cream
generous handful of fresh chopped
chervil, chives or parsley
Wholemeal bread croûtons spread
with cream cheese to serve

1. Melt the butter in a medium-sized saucepan over low heat, then stir in the flour and cook for 1 minute.

2. Pour over the vegetable stock and heat, stirring, to thicken the soup. Add cream cheese, blending well, then add nutmeg, salt, soured cream and herbs. Remove from the heat.

3. Garnish with wholemeal bread croûtons spread with cream cheese.

CHICKEN HOT POT SOUP [P]

1 boiling fowl, jointed
2 carrots, scraped and diced
2 parsnips, peeled and diced
2 celeriac roots, chopped
1 leek, trimmed and sliced
Boiling water to cover
Few green peppercorns
Few juniper berries
Sea salt to taste
1 bay leaf
Chopped chives to garnish

1. Place the boiling fowl, carrots, parsnips, celeriac roots and leek in a large saucepan or pressure cooker and cover with boiling water. Add the green peppercorns, juniper berries, salt and bay leaf. Cook until tender. Remove from the heat.

2. Remove the vegetables and meat with a slotted spoon and strain the stock into a clean saucepan. Skim off the fat. Cut the meat and vegetables into small pieces (discarding the chicken bones) and return to the saucepan. Reheat, remove from the heat and sprinkle generously with chopped chives.

Note: For a richer dish, add some egg (see Stracciatella and Shredded Omelette, page 37).

Note: If celeriac is unavailable, substitute another root vegetable of your choice.

CHICKEN SOUP [P]

1 boiling fowl
2 carrots, scraped and cut into chunks
2 parsnips, peeled and cut into chunks
1 medium-sized onion, chopped
2 stalks celery, chopped
1 bay leaf
Few juniper berries
Water to cover
Chopped parsley to garnish

1. Place the boiling fowl in a large saucepan, add the carrots, parsnips, onion, celery (plus some celery leaves if available), bay leaf and juniper berries. Cover with water.

2. Bring to the boil over moderate heat, skim the stock well, then simmer until the meat is falling off the bones, about 2 hours. Remove from the heat.

3. Strain the soup into a clean saucepan. Cut a few slices of breast meat and add to the saucepan. (The remainder of the chicken meat can be chopped and used in another recipe.) Discard the chicken bones. Chop up the vegetables and add to the soup. Reheat and serve garnished with chopped parsley.

CHINESE LEAVES SOUP [O]

1 head Chinese leaves
1 onion, chopped
½ oz (15g) butter
Vegetable stock *or* water to cover
Few drops soy sauce
Chopped parsley *or* herbs to garnish

1. Shred the Chinese leaves very finely and place in a saucepan with the onion and butter over moderate heat. Sauté for a few minutes, pour over the vegetable stock or water and simmer for about 5 minutes.

2. Remove from the heat and add soy sauce. Garnish with parsley or herbs.

CUCUMBER SOUP [S][P]

1 medium-sized cucumber
1 pint (600ml) lightly salted water
2 cloves garlic, crushed
1 teaspoonful each finely chopped dillweed and borage,
2 tablespoonsful soured cream and a knob of butter *or* 1 cooked potato, peeled and chopped

1. Peel the cucumber if you wish and chop coarsely. Place in a medium-sized saucepan with the water and garlic and cook until cucumber is soft. Remove from the heat, cool slightly and purée in a blender.

2. For a **protein** meal, add dill, borage, soured cream and butter. For a **starch** meal, purée the potato with the cucumber mixture.

FISH STOCK [P]

2 lb (1kg) fish trimmings (heads and tails)
½ lb (225g) root vegetables, diced
1 bay leaf
Pinch of sea salt
Few juniper berries
Few green peppercorns
2½ pints (1.5 litres) water

1. Place all the ingredients in a large saucepan over moderate heat and simmer for one hour. Remove from the heat.

2. Strain the stock, cool and use as the basis for a soup, or freeze in containers or ice cube trays until needed.

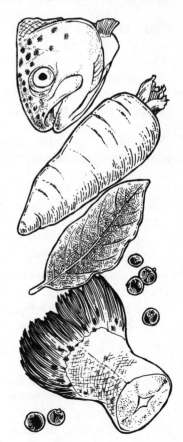

CREAMY FISH SOUP [P]

1 onion, chopped
1-2 Hamburg parsley or celeriac
roots, chopped
1 small aubergine, peeled and
chopped
2 stalks celery, chopped
1 leek, chopped
½ oz (15g) butter
½ lb (225g) white fish fillets
Fish trimmings
A few green peppercorns
1 bay leaf
1 clove
1½ pints (850ml) Vegetable Stock
(page 37)
½ pint (300ml) single cream
1 egg yolk
1 teaspoonful lemon juice
½ teaspoonful potato flour
4 oz (115g) mixed vegetables, cooked
Chopped parsley to garnish

1. Place the onion, Hamburg parsley or
celeriac root, aubergine, celery, leeks and
butter in a large saucepan and sauté
gently over moderate heat. Add the fish
fillets, fish trimmings, peppercorns, bay
leaf, clove, vegetable stock and cream.
Cook gently for about 20 minutes.
Remove from the heat.

2. Remove the fish trimmings with a
slotted spoon, pick out any fish bones
and discard bones and trimmings, dice
the fish fillets and set aside.

3. Purée the soup in a blender. Return to
the rinsed out saucepan and stir in the
egg yolk, lemon juice and soya flour. If
the mixture is too thick, add additional
vegetable stock or water. Reheat the soup
over moderate heat. Add the diced fish
and mixed vegetables. Heat through.

4. Serve in warmed soup bowls
garnished with chopped parsley.

Note: If celeriac is unavailable, substitute
another root vegetable of your choice.

QUICK BOUILLABAISSE [P]

1 leek, trimmed and chopped
2 onions, chopped
2 tablespoonsful cold-pressed olive
oil
1¾ pints (1 litre) water
¼ pint (140ml) dry white wine
½ lb (225g) tomatoes, skinned and
chopped
1 oz (30g) fennel, chopped
1 green pepper, deseeded and
chopped
1 stalk celery, sliced
1 medium-sized carrot, diced
1 clove garlic, chopped
1 teaspoonful finely chopped thyme
2 sprigs parsley, finely chopped
1 bay leaf
Sea salt to taste
Few strands saffron
Few green peppercorns
1 lb (450g) various fish fillets, cut
into chunks

1. Place the leek, onions and oil in a
large saucepan over moderate heat and
sauté until soft, about 5 minutes. Add
water, wine, tomatoes, fennel, green
pepper, celery, carrot, garlic, thyme,
parsley, bay leaf, salt, saffron and green
peppercorns. Simmer for about 30
minutes.

2. Add fish fillets and cook until just
done, about 5-10 minutes.

SPANISH FISH SOUP [P]

2 onions, chopped
2 tablespoonsful cold-pressed olive
oil
1 lb (450g) fish fillets, diced
2 cloves garlic, chopped
Dry white wine to cover
Pinch of sea salt
Few green peppercorns
1 bay leaf
½ lb (225g) tomatoes, skinned and
coarsely chopped
1½ pints (900ml) Vegetable Stock
(page 37)
1 tablespoonful potato flour
3 tablespoonsful dry white wine
Grated Parmesan cheese to garnish
Chopped chives to garnish

1. Place the onions and oil in a large
saucepan over moderate heat and sauté
until soft, about 5 minutes. Add fish
fillets and garlic and still well.

2. Pour over enough wine to cover, add
salt, peppercorns and bay leaf and cook
gently for 5 minutes.

3. Remove fish from the soup with a
slotted spoon and divide between the
soup bowls. Set aside.

4. Add tomatoes and vegetable stock to
the saucepan, bring to the boil, then
thicken with the flour, mixed to a paste
with the wine. Cook through, divide
between the soup plates and garnish
with grated cheese and chives.

JERUSALEM ARTICHOKE SOUP [S]

1lb (450g) Jerusalem artichokes
2 tablespoonsful chopped parsley
½ oz (15g) butter
1 tablespoonful potato flour
2 pints (1 litre) Vegetable Stock
(page 37)
Wholemeal bread croûtons to
garnish
Chopped basil or chives to garnish

1. Peel and dice the Jerusalem artichokes
and place in a medium-sized saucepan
with the parsley and butter. Sauté gently
over moderate heat, stir in the flour and
cook for 1 minute.

2. Pour over the vegetable stock and
cook until the artichokes are tender.
Remove from the heat.

3. Garnish with wholemeal bread
croûtons and chopped basil or chives.

LEEK SOUP [S]

4 leeks, trimmed and sliced
1¾ pints (1 litre) lightly salted water
1 raw potato, peeled (optional)
Knob of butter
Handful of chopped dillweed
Soured cream to serve

1. Cook the leeks in the salted water
until tender. Remove from the heat.

2. Purée the mixture in a blender, if
desired, or grate a potato into the stock
to thicken.

3. Stir in a knob of butter and serve
sprinkled with chopped dillweed and a
spoonful of soured cream.

Onion Soup [S]

4 medium-sized onions
1 tablespoonful corn oil
1¾ pints (1 litre) boiling water
Pinch of sea salt
4 slices wholemeal bread
1 clove garlic
Butter and cream cheese to spread
Dash of dry white wine
Paprika and chopped chives to serve

1. Cut the onions into fine rings. Heat the oil in a medium-sized saucepan over moderate heat and sauté the onions until soft, but do not let them brown. Add the boiling water and salt and simmer until the onions are soft.

2. Meanwhile, rub the bread slices with the garlic and spread with butter and cream cheese. Heat the grill and toast the bread, spread side up.

3. When the soup is ready, remove from the heat, add a dash of wine and pour into soup plates. Float the toast on top and sprinkle with paprika and chopped chives.

Fresh Pea Soup [S]

2 lb (900g) fresh peas, shelled
2 pints (1 litre) Vegetable Stock (page 37)
1 tablespoonful wholemeal flour
⅓ oz (10g) butter
Chopped parsley or basil to garnish

1. Place the peas and vegetable stock in a medium-sixed saucepan and cook over moderate heat until soft. Remove from the heat.

2. Make a roux with the flour and butter and add gradually to the soup to thicken. Cook for a further 5 minutes.

3. For a smooth consistency, purée the peas with the stock in a blender, reserving some whole peas for garnish.

4. Garnish with chopped parsley or basil.

Cream of Potato Soup [S]

1 pint (600ml) Vegetable Stock (page 37)
½ lb (225g) floury potatoes, peeled
⅓ oz (10g) butter
1 tablespoonful finely chopped dillweed
2½ fl oz (75ml) soured cream
1 egg yolk
Chopped dillweed to garnish

1. Bring the vegetable stock to the boil in a medium-sized saucepan. Reduce the heat to a simmer, add the potatoes and cook until soft. Remove from the heat and purée in a blender.

2. Melt the butter in a medium-sized saucepan, stir in the dillweed and cook briefly to soften. Pour the potato purée into the saucepan, stir to mix and heat through. Remove from the heat.

3. Combine the soured cream and egg yolk in a cup, stir into the soup and serve immediately, sprinkled with chopped dillweed.

COUNTRY-STYLE RICE SOUP S

3 tablespoonsful brown rice
1 carrot, scraped and diced
1 stalk celery, diced
1 celeriac root, chopped
Fresh chopped thyme to taste
1¾ pints (1 litre) lightly salted water
1 egg yolk
1½ tablespoonsful soured cream
Finely chopped chives to garnish

1. Place the rice, carrot, celery, celeriac root, thyme and water in a medium-sized saucepan and cook over moderate heat until the rice is very soft and glutinous and the vegetables are soft. Remove from the heat.

2. Combine the egg yolk and soured cream in a soup tureen and pour the soup over, stirring constantly.

3. Serve sprinkled with chopped chives.

Note: If celeriac is unavailable, substitute another root vegetable of your choice.

TOMATO SOUP P

2 lb (900g) ripe tomatoes, skinned and chopped
1½ pints (900ml) Vegetable Stock (page 37)
Sea salt to taste
Pinch of thyme
Pinch of paprika
½ teaspoonful potato flour (optional)

1. Purée the tomatoes in a blender.

2. Place the tomatoes and vegetable stock in a medium-sized saucepan over moderate heat and cook until hot. Remove from the heat.

3. Season with salt, thyme and paprika. Thicken, if desired, with the potato flour, mixed to a paste with a little water.

RAW TOMATO SOUP O

2 lb (900g) ripe tomatoes
Sea salt to taste
2 tablespoonsful finely chopped parsley
1 tablespoonful chopped basil
Few drops soy sauce

1. Skin the tomatoes and cut out the tough bit at the stalk end. Discard.

2. Chop the tomatoes roughly and purée in a blender until smooth, thinning the tomato purée with a little water if necessary.

3. Season with salt, parsley, basil and soy sauce. Chill if desired. This is a very thirst-quenching soup.

COLD VEGETABLE- [P]
YOGURT SOUP

1 green pepper, deseeded and
chopped
½ cucumber, chopped
1 small onion, chopped
2 cloves garlic, chopped
1 small kohlrabi bulb, diced
2 teaspoonsful cold-pressed olive oil
Few drops of cider vinegar
8 fl oz (240ml) yogurt or buttermilk
1 tomato, skinned and diced
Chopped fresh chervil, dill or chives
to garnish

1. Place the pepper, cucumber, onion,
garlic, kohlrabi, oil and vinegar in a
blender container and blend until
puréed, but not entirely smooth.

2. Pour the yogurt or buttermilk into a
serving bowl and add the vegetable
purée. Mix well, then chill in the
refrigerator until needed.

3. To serve, pour the soup into
individual bowls and garnish with diced
tomato and chopped herbs.

CREAM OF [S]
VEGETABLE SOUP

1 lb (450g) seasonal vegetables,
coarsely chopped
1¾ pints (1 litre) water
Few spinach or lettuce leaves
2 teaspoonsful wholemeal flour
Knob of butter or 1 tablespoonful
soured cream
Chopped parsley or chervil to
garnish

1. Place the vegetables and water in a
large saucepan over moderate heat, bring
to the boil, cover and simmer gently
until tender, about 25 minutes. Remove
from the heat and cool slightly.

2. Purée in a blender with a few spinach
or lettuce leaves and the flour.

3. Return the soup to the saucepan and
heat through.

4. To serve, stir in the butter or soured
cream and sprinkle with chopped parsley
or chervil.

HEARTY VEGETABLE ⒮ SOUP

2 carrots, scraped and diced
2 stalks celery, diced
2 Hamburg parsley *or* celeriac roots, diced
Few white or green cabbage leaves, shredded
1-2 leeks, trimmed and sliced
1¾ pints (1 litre) Vegetable Stock (page 37)
Sea salt to taste
3 cloves garlic, crushed with a little sea salt
Thinly sliced wholemeal bread
2 tablespoonsful sunflower oil
1 egg yolk
Dillweed, chervil *or* parsley to garnish
Soured cream to serve

1. Place the carrots, celery, Hamburg parsley or celeriac roots, cabbage, leeks and vegetable stock in a large saucepan and cook over moderate heat until the vegetables are tender, but not too soft. Remove from the heat, season with salt and keep warm.

2. Spread the garlic-salt mixture on the bread, pressing it down well.

3. Heat the oil in a large frying pan and sauté the bread briefly on both sides. Remove from the heat and place 1 slice of bread in the bottom of each soup plate.

3. Stir the egg yolk into the soup, then pour over the bread. Serve immediately, garnished with dillweed, chervil or parsley and a spoonful of soured cream.

Note: If celeriac is unavailable, substitute another root vegetable of your choice.

FARMHOUSE ⒮⒫⒪ VEGETABLE SOUP

2 carrots, scraped
2 parsnips, peeled
1 small cauliflower
2 stalks celery
4 tomatoes, skinned and coarsely chopped *or* ½ lb (225g) mushrooms, coarsely chopped
1¾ pints (1 litre) water
Pinch of sea salt
1 potato, cooked and peeled (optional)
Knob of butter
Fresh chopped herbs to garnish

1. Cut the carrots and parsnips into julienne strips, separate the cauliflower into florets and slice the celery. Place in a large saucepan with the tomatoes (for a **protein** meal) or mushrooms (for a **starch** or **neutral** recipe) and water. Add salt and bring to the boil, then simmer gently until tender.

2. Thicken the soup by puréeing in a blender with potato, for a **starch** meal, or leave as is for a **protein** or **neutral** recipe, add a knob of butter and sprinkle with fresh chopped herbs.

Note: This soup can be made with a combination of any seasonal vegetables, but take care when using tomatoes, as they will be cooked. If you are planning to follow the soup with a **starch** meal, you should not add tomatoes to your soup.

RAW VEGETABLE SOUP [O]

1 stalk celery, chopped
1 carrot, scraped and chopped
1 parsnip, chopped
2 cabbage leaves, chopped
1 leek, trimmed and chopped
1 tomato, skinned and chopped
½ pint (300ml) water
1¼ pints (750ml) Vegetable Stock
(page 37)
Chopped fresh herbs
Knob of butter
Soured cream to serve (optional)

1. Place all the vegetables in a blender container with the water and blend to a purée.

2. Bring the vegetable stock to a boil, remove from the heat and stir in the vegetable purée, chopped herbs and butter. Stir well.

3. Serve with a dollop of soured cream on top, if wished.

FRENCH WATERCRESS SOUP [S]

1 onion, finely chopped
½ oz (15g) butter
1 bunch watercress, stalks removed
1¾ pints (1 litre) Vegetable Stock
(page 37)
Pinch of sea salt
1 raw potato, peeled
Pinch of grated nutmeg
1½ tablespoonsful soured cream
Few drops soy sauce

1. Place the onion and butter in a medium-sized saucepan and sauté over moderate heat until soft.

2. Add half the watercress to the saucepan and cook gently until soft. Pour over the vegetable stock and cook briefly until heated. Add salt, grate the potato into the soup and remove from the heat.

3. Season the soup with nutmeg, soured cream and soy sauce, then stir in the remaining watercress.

VEGETABLES

The best vegetables are those grown in your own garden, or by a farmer you trust to use only organic fertilizers. Look first for freshness — make sure that greens are not limp, that cauliflower is firm and white and that root vegetables are hard and crisp. Only really fresh vegetables contain the full complement of vitamins.

Vegetables should be steamed briefly in very little water. Use the water left behind in the pan for vegetable stocks or other dishes. Frying and cooking in batter should be avoided if possible — it is much better to serve vegetables in their natural state. Add butter to the cooked vegetable, rather than using it as a cooking medium. This way, vegetables are healthier and more easily digested.

A freezer will help you provide for the winter months when fresh vegetables are difficult to come by and those out of season are expensive.

SAUTÉED AUBERGINES ⃞O

2 tablespoonsful cold-pressed olive
oil
1¼ lb (565g) aubergines, peeled and
diced
1 tablespoonful chopped lemon
balm
1 tablespoonful chopped parsley
1 teaspoonful chopped marjoram *or*
oregano
1 teaspoonful chopped thyme
Sea salt and freshly ground black
pepper to taste
¼ pint (140ml) soured cream
Finely chopped dillweed to garnish

1. Heat the oil in a large frying pan over
moderate heat.

2. Add the aubergines, herbs, salt and
pepper and sauté gently until tender.

3. Stir in the soured cream and heat
through.

4. To serve, sprinkle with finely chopped
dillweed.

STUFFED AUBERGINES ⃞P

2 medium-sized aubergines
2 tablespoonsful cold-pressed olive
oil
4 oz (115g) minced beef *or* chicken
1 egg, beaten
1 medium-sized onion, finely
chopped
1 tablespoonful finely chopped
parsley
1 teaspoonful chopped rosemary
1 clove garlic, crushed
1 teaspoonful chopped marjoram *or*
oregano
Sea salt and freshly ground black
pepper to taste

Sauce:
2 teaspoonsful cold-pressed olive oil
1 onion, finely chopped
4 medium-sized tomatoes, skinned
and chopped
Pinch of sea salt and freshly ground
black pepper
Handful of basil leaves, chopped
1 clove garlic, crushed
2 oz (55g) grated Parmesan cheese

1. Cut the aubergines in half lengthways
and carefully scoop out the flesh. Chop
the flesh coarsely, reserving the shells.

2. Heat the oil in a large frying pan over
moderate heat. Add the aubergine flesh
and cook gently until almost tender.

3. In a bowl, mix the aubergine flesh,
minced beef or chicken, egg, onion,
parsley, rosemary, garlic, marjoram or
oregano, salt and pepper. Stuff the
aubergine shells with this mixture.

4. Preheat the oven to 350°F/180°C (Gas
Mark 4).

5. Prepare the sauce. Heat the oil in a medium-sized saucepan over moderate heat and sauté the onion until soft, about 5 minutes. Stir in the tomatoes, salt, pepper, basil and garlic. Cook gently for 5 minutes, then remove from the heat.

6. Place the stuffed aubergines in an overproof dish that will hold them in one layer. Pour the sauce over, sprinkle with grated cheese, cover the dish with a lid or aluminium foil and bake for 1 hour.

7. Serve hot.

STEAMED BROCCOLI [O]

1½ lb (675g) broccoli
Melted butter to serve
Finely chopped garlic to garnish

1. Cut off the tough, woody parts of the broccoli stems and discard. Peel the remaining stems and if they are large, cut in half lengthways.

2. Place the stems in a steamer basket that will fit inside a saucepan. Fill the saucepan with a very small amount of lightly salted water and bring to the boil over moderate heat. Place the steamer basket in the saucepan, cover tightly and steam for 5 minutes. Add the broccoli florets to the steamer, cover the saucepan again and steam until the broccoli is just tender. Remove from the heat.

3. Take the steamer out of the saucepan carefully and place the broccoli in a warmed serving dish. Toss gently with melted butter and garnish with finely chopped garlic.

CABBAGE HOTPOT [S]

1 lb (450g) white cabbage, coarsely shredded
1 lb (450g) potatoes, peeled and diced
1 teaspoonful cumin seeds
Few sprigs of wild thyme or other herb, finely chopped
2 tablespoonsful soured cream
1 tablespoonful wholemeal flour

1. Place the cabbage, potatoes, cumin seeds and herbs in a large saucepan with about ½ pint (300ml) lightly salted water. Place over moderate heat and cook until the vegetables are almost done.

2. Stir together the soured cream and flour and add to the pan. When the sauce has thickened, remove from the heat serve.

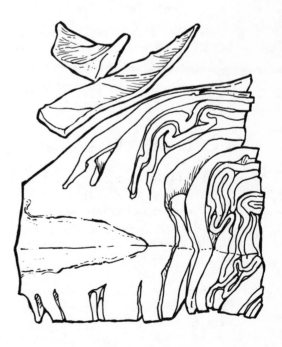

STUFFED CABBAGE LEAVES S

12 cabbage leaves

Filling:
4 oz (115g) brown rice, cooked
½ lb (225g) fresh or frozen peas
Sea salt to taste
1 teaspoonful finely chopped marjoram
Butter to grease
Vegetable Stock to cover (page 37)
Soured cream to serve

1. Blanch the cabbage leaves in boiling water. Drain and beat the tough ribs with a meat mallet until soft. Set aside.

2. Make the filling. Mix together the rice, peas, salt and marjoram. Divide the filling between the cabbage leaves, roll up and fit snugly into a greased flameproof dish, seam side down.

3. Heat the vegetable stock, pour over the stuffed cabbage leaves, place over low heat and cook for 20-30 minutes.

4. To serve, top each cabbage roll with a little soured cream.

STEAMED CARROTS O

1 lb (450g) carrots, scraped
Sea salt to taste
1 teaspoonful cumin seeds
2 tablespoonsful chopped parsley
2 tablespoonsful soured cream *or*
½ oz (15g) butter

1. Cut the carrots into julienne strips. Place in a medium-sized saucepan with very little water, salt and cumin seeds. Cover and cook over moderate heat until the carrots are tender and most of the

water has been absorbed. Remove from the heat.

2. To serve, sprinkle with chopped parsley and stir in the soured cream or butter.

STEAMED CAULIFLOWER O

1 large whole cauliflower, trimmed
Melted butter to serve
Chopped parsley to garnish

1. Soak the cauliflower in a pan of lightly salted water for 30 minutes, then drain and discard water.

2. Place the whole cauliflower in a steamer basket which will fit into a saucepan. Fill the saucepan with very little lightly salted water and bring to the boil over moderate heat. Place the steamer basket into the saucepan, cover tightly and steam until tender, about 20 minutes. Remove from the heat.

3. Take the steamer out of the saucepan carefully and place the cauliflower on a warmed serving plate. Pour over some melted butter and sprinkle with parsley.

CAULIFLOWER BAKE ☐O

Butter to grease
1 steamed cauliflower (page 52)
separated into florets
2 tablespoonsful finely chopped
parsley *or* basil
2 egg yolks
½ pint (300ml) soured cream

1. Preheat the oven to 350°F/180°C (Gas Mark 4). Grease an ovenproof dish with butter.

2. Place the cauliflower in the dish, sprinkling each layer with chopped parsley or basil.

3. Whisk together the egg yolks and soured cream and pour over the cauliflower. Bake for 20 minutes, until the sauce is bubbling and the cauliflower is cooked.

CAULIFLOWER PURÉE ☐S

1 medium-sized cauliflower
½ lb (225g) floury potatoes
1 tablespoonful soured cream
Sea salt to taste
½ teaspoonful ground cumin seeds
Pinch of grated nutmeg
1 egg yolk
Knob of butter
Paprika

1. Steam the cauliflower until quite soft (see page 52). Reserve the cooking water. Meanwhile, boil the potatoes until tender, drain and peel.

2. Purée the cauliflower and potatoes in a blender, adding the soured cream and enough of the cauliflower cooking water to obtain the right consistency. Season

with salt, cumin and nutmeg, stir in the egg yolk and butter.

3. Preheat the oven to 350°F/180°C (Gas Mark 4). Grease an ovenproof dish with a little additional butter, turn the purée into the dish, dust with paprika and bake until heated through.

CAULIFLOWER IN WHITE SAUCE ☐S

1 steamed cauliflower (page 52),
separated into florets, ¼ pint (140ml)
cooking water reserved
½ oz (15g) butter
1 tablespoonful wholemeal flour
2 teaspoonsful soured cream
2 tablespoonsful finely chopped
parsley *or* other herbs

1. Melt the butter in a medium-sized saucepan over moderate heat. Stir in the flour and cook for 1 minute. Pour in the cauliflower cooking water and heat through, then add the cauliflower florets. Remove from the heat.

2. Stir in the soured cream and sprinkle with parsley or herbs before serving.

SAUTÉED CELERIAC ▢

**1 large celeriac root, leaves reserved
and chopped
1 oz (30g) butter
Sea salt and freshly ground black
pepper to taste**

1. Scrub the celeriac well, remove the leaves and reserve. Steam the root, whole, in its skin over boiling salted water until soft. Remove from the heat and cool slightly.

2. Cut the celeriac root into thick slices.

3. Melt the butter in a large frying pan over moderate heat and sauté the celeriac slices until golden. Remove from the heat and sprinkle with chopped celeriac leaves and season with salt and pepper.

4. Serve hot.

CELERIAC AND CARROT PURÉE ▢

**¾ lb (340g) celeriac, peeled and
diced, leaves reserved
¾ lb (340g) carrots, scraped and
sliced
1 tablespoonful finely chopped fresh
herbs
Sea salt and freshly ground black
pepper to taste**

1. Cook the celeriac and carrots separately in a very little salted water until tender. Drain, reserving the cooking juices. Cool slightly.

2. Purée the celeriac and carrots in a blender, in batches if necessary, adding enough of the cooking juices to obtain a smooth consistency.

3. Turn the purée into a saucepan. Chop the celeriac leaves finely and add to the purée with herbs, salt and pepper.

4. Reheat gently over low heat, whisking the mixture until it is light and fluffy. Serve hot.

SAUTÉED CELERY ▢

**1 head celery, leaves reserved
1 oz (30g) butter
1 tablespoonful finely chopped
parsley
1 tablespoonful soured cream**

1. Wash the celery well to remove all grit. Divide into stalks and blanch in lightly salted boiling water for about 5 minutes. Drain.

2. Meanwhile, chop the celery leaves finely.

3. Cut the celery stalks into 4-inch (10cm) lengths.

4. Melt the butter in a large frying pan over moderate heat. Add the celery, chopped leaves and parsley and sauté until the celery is tender.

5. Just before serving, stir in the soured cream.

STUFFED COURGETTES [P]

**4 large courgettes, scrubbed
2 oz (55g) soya bean sprouts
4 oz (115g) cooked minced beef *or*
chicken
1 medium-sized onion, finely
chopped
1 egg, beaten
Pinch of sea salt and freshly ground
black pepper
1 pint (600ml) Vegetable Stock
(page 37)**

1. Cut the courgettes in half lengthways and remove the flesh, being careful to leave the shells intact. Set the shells aside and chop the flesh into a bowl.

2. Add the bean sprouts, beef or chicken, onion, egg, salt and pepper to the bowl and mix well. Stuff the courgette shells with this mixture.

3. Place the vegetable stock into a large shallow pan that will hold the courgettes in one layer, add the stuffed courgettes and bring to the boil over moderate heat. Reduce the heat and simmer, covered, until the courgettes are tender. Serve hot.

SPRING GREENS WITH PEAS [S]

**1 bunch spring greens
1 tablespoonful butter
1 medium-sized onion, chopped
1 tablespoonful wholemeal flour
½ lb (225g) fresh *or* frozen peas
Pinch of grated nutmeg
1 clove garlic, crushed
Soured cream to serve**

1. Trim and wash the greens. Cook in lightly salted boiling water until tender, drain well, reserving the cooking water and chop finely.

2. Melt the butter in a medium-sized saucepan over moderate heat, add the onion and cook gently until transparent. Stir in the flour and cook 1 minute. Pour over the cooking water from the greens and cook until the sauce has thickened.

3. Add the peas, nutmeg and garlic. Stir in the chopped greens and heat through.

4. Stir in a little soured cream just before serving.

STEAMED KOHLRABI [S]

**1½ lb (675g) kohlrabi, peeled and
diced, leaves reserved
1 medium-sized onion, finely
chopped
Handful of fresh mint, chopped
2 tablespoonsful chopped chervil
Pinch of grated nutmeg
1 lovage leaf
1 natural vegetable stock cube,
crumbled (optional)
Sea salt and freshly ground black
pepper to taste
Knob of butter**

1. Place the kohlrabi and very little lightly salted water in a medium-sized saucepan and steam, covered, over moderate heat. Meanwhile, chop the kohlrabi leaves.

2. Halfway through the cooking time, add the onion, mint, chervil, kohlrabi leaves, nutmeg and lovage. Continue cooking until the kohlrabi is soft. Remove from the heat.

3. To serve, season with salt and pepper, add a knob of butter and mix lightly.

KOHLRABI PURÉE [S]

¾ lb (340g) kohlrabi, peeled and
diced, leaves reserved
¾ lb (340g) cooked potatoes
Knob of butter
1 tablespoonful finely chopped
parsley
1 teaspoonful finely chopped chervil

1. Steam the kohlrabi in a very little
salted water until soft (see previous
recipe). Meanwhile, chop the kohlrabi
leaves finely.

2. Purée the kohlrabi and potatoes
together in a blender. Add the butter,
kohlrabi leaves, parsley and chervil and
beat well until the mixture is light and
fluffy.

3. Return the mixture to a saucepan and
heat through.

LEEKS WITH SOURED [S] CREAM

1 lb (450g) leeks, trimmed
1 tablespoonful corn oil
¼ pint (140ml) vegetable stock *or*
water
Wholemeal flour
1 clove garlic, crushed
1 tablespoonful soured cream

1. Slice the leeks thinly into rings.

2. Heat the oil in a saucepan over low
heat, add the leeks and cook for about 5
minutes. Pour over the vegetable stock or
water and continue cooking until soft.
Remove from the heat.

3. Dust the leeks with a little flour and
return to the heat to cook through.

4. Just before serving, add the garlic and
stir in the soured cream.

SAUTÉED PEPPERS [O]

1 green pepper, deseeded
1 yellow pepper, deseeded
1 red pepper, deseeded
½ oz (15g) butter
Sea salt and freshly ground black
pepper to taste

1. Cut the peppers into julienne strips.

2. Melt the butter in a medium-sized
frying pan over moderate heat. Add the
peppers and sauté gently until soft.
Season with salt and pepper.

PUMPKIN BAKE [S]

2 lb (900g) pumpkin
Wholemeal flour
1 oz (30g) butter
6 large cloves garlic
1 handful parsley *or* dillweed, finely
chopped
Pinch of sea salt and freshly ground
black pepper

1. Preheat the oven to 350°F/180°C (Gas
Mark 4).

2. Remove the seeds and fibre from the
pumpkin and dice the flesh. Toss in
wholemeal flour to coat lightly.

3. Grease an ovenproof dish with some
of the butter and add the pumpkin,
garlic, parsley or dillweed, salt and
pepper.

4. Dot with the remaining butter. (Do
not be tempted to add any liquid as
pumpkin contains a lot of water.)

5. Bake in the oven for about 30 minutes. Serve hot.

STEAMED PUMPKIN WITH SOURED CREAM SAUCE ⒮

2 lb (900g) pumpkin
Pinch of sea salt and freshly ground black pepper
1 teaspoonful cumin seeds
¼ pint (140ml) soured cream
1 tablespoonful wholemeal flour
Finely chopped dillweed to serve
1 clove garlic, crushed to serve

1. Remove the seeds and fibre from the pumpkin and dice the flesh.

2. Place the pumpkin in a saucepan with very little water (pumpkin contains a lot of water) with the salt, pepper and cumin seeds and cook, covered, over moderate heat until the pumpkin is tender.

3. Mix together the soured cream and flour and add to the pan. Cook through briefly, stirring well to mix.

4. To serve, sprinkle with finely chopped dillweed and crushed garlic.

CREAMED SPINACH ⒮

1 onion, finely chopped
½ oz (15g) butter
1 lb (450g) fresh spinach, tough stalks removed
Sea salt and freshly ground black pepper to taste
Pinch of grated nutmeg
1 clove garlic, finely chopped
1 tablespoonful wholemeal flour
4 tablespoonsful soured cream
1 egg yolk

1. Cook the onion with the butter in a small saucepan over low heat until transparent. Remove from the heat.

2. Place the onion in a blender with the spinach, salt and pepper, nutmeg, garlic and flour and purée.

3. Turn the mixture into a medium-sized saucepan and cook through briefly.

5. Meanwhile, mix together the soured cream and egg yolk. When the spinach is cooked, stir in the soured cream mixture and serve immediately.

SPINACH DUMPLINGS [P]

**1 lb (450g) fresh spinach
1½ oz (40g) Ricotta cheese
2 tablespoonsful grated Parmesan
cheese
1 egg yolk
1 clove garlic, very finely chopped
Pinch of sea salt and freshly ground
black pepper
¼ teaspoonful grated nutmeg
2 egg whites
Butter to grease
Tomato Sauce (page 100) to serve**

1. Wash the spinach well. Place in a covered saucepan over medium-high heat without adding any more water than is clinging to the leaves and cook for 3-5 minutes, stirring once halfway through the cooking time. Remove from the heat, drain and rinse in cold water.

2. Squeeze out excess moisture, then chop finely. Place the spinach in a bowl. Add the Ricotta and Parmesan cheese, egg yolk, garlic, salt, pepper and nutmeg. Set aside.

3. Bring a large saucepan of lightly salted water to the boil. Reduce to a simmer.

4. Meanwhile, whisk the egg whites with a wire whisk in a deep bowl, preferably a copper one, until stiff, but not dry. Stir some of the egg whites into the spinach mixture to lighten it, then fold in the remaining egg whites, using a figure-of-eight motion.

5. To make the dumplings, dip a teaspoon into the simmering water and fill with the spinach mixture. Dip another teaspoon into the water and invert over the first spoon to form an egg-shaped dumpling. Slide each dumpling into the simmering water, using the second teaspoon as a pusher.

Continue to form the dumplings, dropping them into the simmering water, but avoid overcrowding the pan. Cook for about 2 minutes on each side, then remove with a slotted spoon and drain on absorbent kitchen paper.

6. To keep the dumplings warm, grease an ovenproof dish and arrange the dumplings in it. Place in a 225°F/100°C (Gas Mark ¼) oven until all the dumplings have been poached and drained.

7. Serve with Tomato Sauce, float in vegetable, chicken or fish stock, or serve with a thin soup.

ROMANIAN TOMATOES [P]

**2 green peppers, deseeded
2 red peppers, deseeded
1 medium-sized onion
2 tablespoonsful cold-pressed olive
oil
10-12 ripe tomatoes, skinned
1 small chilli pepper, very finely
chopped (optional)
Sea salt and freshly ground black
pepper to taste
Finely chopped parsley *or* chervil to
garnish**

1. Cut the green and red peppers into julienne strips. Slice the onion finely.

2. Heat the oil in a large saucepan over moderate heat. Add the peppers and onion, reduce the heat and cook gently for about 25 minutes.

3. Meanwhile, chop the tomatoes coarsely. Add to the vegetables in the pan and cook for a further 10 minutes, adding the chopped chilli, if using. Season with salt and pepper and serve

sprinkled with finely chopped parsley or chervil.

SAUTÉED TOMATOES $\boxed{\text{P}}$

**1 lb (450g) ripe tomatoes
Sea salt and freshly ground black
pepper to taste
2 tablespoonsful corn oil
Finely chopped parsley *or* chervil to
garnish**

1. Cut the tomatoes in half crossways. Sprinkle with salt and pepper.

2. Heat the oil in a medium-sized frying pan over moderate heat. Add the tomatoes, cut-side down and sauté gently, about 5 minutes. Turn the tomatoes and continue cooking for another 5 minutes, or until they are nice and soft. Remove from the heat.

3. To serve, sprinkle with finely chopped parsley or chervil.

CASSEROLED VEGETABLES WITH BUCKWHEAT $\boxed{\text{S}}$

**1½ lb (675g) assorted raw vegetables
in season
Sea salt
Handful of chopped parsley
Chopped fresh savory to taste
½ lb (225g) buckwheat
1 egg yolk
¼ pint (140ml) soured cream
Pinch of grated nutmeg, chopped
thyme *or* marjoram**

1. Prepare a römertopf (chicken brick) by soaking it in cold water for 30 minutes.

2. Meanwhile, cut up the vegetables, sprinkle with salt, parsley and savory and set aside.

3. Cook the buckwheat in salted water until tender.

4. Preheat the oven to 350°F/180°C (Gas Mark 4). Layer the vegetables and buckwheat in the casserole.

5. Combine the egg yolk and soured cream and season with nutmeg, thyme or marjoram. Pour over the vegetable mixture, cover, and bake in the oven for about 20 minutes.

Vegetable-Cheese Bake [P]

1 large aubergine
Sea salt
2 onions, sliced
1 red pepper, deseeded
1 green pepper, deseeded
1 yellow pepper, deseeded
1 oz (30g) butter
4 small tomatoes, skinned
2 eggs
3 tablespoonsful soured cream
2 oz (55g) Feta cheese, crumbled
Chopped chives to garnish

1. Peel the aubergine, slice and sprinkle with sea salt. Set aside for 15 minutes.

2. Meanwhile, cut the red, green and yellow peppers into julienne strips.

3. Squeeze the bitter juices from the aubergine and pat dry with absorbent kitchen paper.

4. Melt the butter in a flameproof casserole over low heat, add the aubergine, onions and peppers and cook gently for 10-15 minutes. Cut the tomatoes into quarters and add to the mixture; cook briefly. Remove from the heat.

5. Preheat the oven to 350°F/180°C (Gas Mark 4).

6. Beat together the eggs, soured cream and a pinch of salt in a bowl. Pour over the vegetables, sprinkle with feta cheese and bake for 20 minutes. Garnish with chopped chives.

Vegetable Ragoût [S][P][O]

1½ lb (675g) assorted raw vegetables, cut into chunks (kohlrabi, celery, carrots, French beans, green or red pepper, pumpkin)
1 onion, finely chopped
Handful of finely chopped parsley
Handful of celery leaves
1 tablespoonful chopped thyme
1 tablespoonful chopped lovage
½ teaspoonful ground cumin seeds
½ teaspoonful paprika
Sea salt to taste
2 cloves garlic, crushed

For a starch meal, add:
1 raw potato, peeled
2 teaspoonsful soured cream

1. Place all ingredients except the garlic and the **starch** additions into a large saucepan with very little water and cook gently, covered, over moderate heat until tender.

2. Just before the vegetables are ready, add the crushed garlic. For a **protein** or **neutral** meal, serve as is. For a **starch** meal, grate the potato into the mixture to thicken it, heat through, remove from the heat and stir in the soured cream.

Winter Vitamin Hotpot S

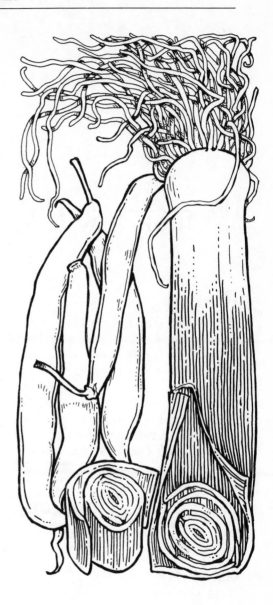

1 celeriac root, peeled and diced
2 carrots, scraped and diced
1 kohlrabi bulb, peeled and diced
4 oz (115g) fresh *or* frozen French
beans
4 oz (115g) fresh *or* frozen peas
½ small cabbage, chopped
1 onion, chopped
1 leek, trimmed and sliced
2 potatoes, diced
Butter *or* soured cream to serve
Sea salt and freshly ground black
pepper to taste
Finely chopped herbs to garnish

1. Cook the celeriac, carrots and kohlrabi in a large saucepan in very little lightly salted water until half-cooked.

2. Add the beans, peas, cabbage, onion, leek and potatoes and continue to cook until all the vegetables are tender. Remove from the heat.

3. Stir in a little butter or soured cream, season with salt and pepper and sprinkle with herbs. Serve immediately.

Note: If celeriac is unavailable, substitute another root vegetable of your choice.

POTATOES, PASTA AND GRAINS

POTATOES

Potatoes are high in carbohydrates; anyone following the Hay System of eating should not eat them at protein meals.

The potato is often regarded as the 'ugly sister' among vegetables. It is also often accused of being fattening — quite unfairly, because it will only make you fat if it is consistently eaten in large quantities, or with a great deal of butter or soured cream.

Potatoes are in fact a very versatile staple food, rich in vitamin C, but although there are countless ways of serving them, they are usually dished up the same way.

When serving potatoes, it is preferable to leave the skin on during cooking (boiling or baking), so that as much natural goodness as possible is retained.

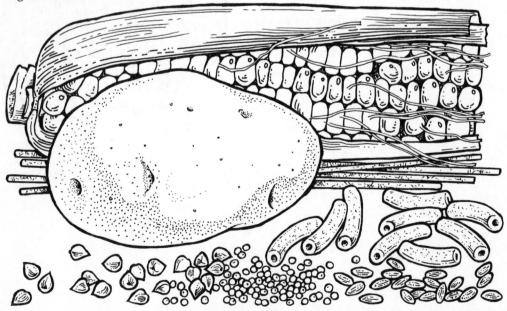

POTATOES BIRCHER-BENNER [S]

2 lb (900g) medium-sized potatoes
Corn oil to grease
Sea salt and freshly ground black
pepper to taste
1 teaspoonful cumin seeds

1. Preheat the oven to 400°F/200°C (Gas Mark 6).

2. Wash the potatoes, scrubbing their skins well, then dry and cut in half lengthways.

3. Oil a baking sheet. Sprinkle the potatoes with salt, pepper and cumin seeds and place cut-side down on the baking sheet. Bake for about 30 minutes, or until tender.

MARJORAM POTATOES [S]

2 lb (900g) potatoes
½ oz (15g) butter
2 tablespoonsful wholemeal flour
⅓ pint (210ml) Vegetable Stock
(page 37)
Handful of fresh marjoram, very
finely chopped
Freshly ground black pepper
Soured cream to serve (optional)

1. Cook the potatoes in their skins until tender. Drain and set aside.

2. Melt the butter in a medium-sized saucepan over moderate heat. Stir in the flour and cook 1 minute, then add the vegetable stock, stirring until the sauce thickens. Remove from the heat.

3. Slice the potatoes into the sauce, add the marjoram and pepper to taste and reheat over low heat.

4. Serve with a dollop of soured cream for special occasions.

Variations:
Use the above method, but substitute dill for the majoram.

BAKED POTATOES WITH HERB BUTTER [S]

4 large baking potatoes
1 oz (30g) butter
Sea salt and freshly ground black
pepper to taste
Finely chopped dill, chervil, basil *or*
parsley

1. Preheat the oven to 400°F/200°C (Gas Mark 6).

2. Wash the potatoes, scrubbing their skins well, then dry well. Bake in the oven for about an hour.

3. When the potatoes are done, cut a slit in each potato, insert a portion of the butter and sprinkle with salt, pepper and finely chopped herbs.

POTATO RAGOÛT [S]

1½ lb (680g) potatoes
4 carrots, scraped and cut into large
chunks
3 stalks celery, sliced
1 pint (600ml) Vegetable Stock
(page 37)
Pinch of sea salt
1 onion, finely chopped
1 teaspoonful cumin seeds
1 bay leaf
1 tablespoonful finely chopped
thyme
1 teaspoonful very finely chopped
fresh chilli pepper
Pinch of cayenne pepper
Wholemeal flour to thicken
(optional)
Soured cream to serve (optional)
Chopped chervil to garnish

1. Wash the potatoes, scrubbing their
skins well and cut into large chunks.

2. Place the potatoes, carrots, celery,
vegetable stock, salt, onion, cumin seeds,
bay leaf, thyme, chilli and cayenne
peppers in a medium-sized saucepan and
bring to the boil over moderate heat.
Reduce heat and cook gently until
potatoes and vegetables are tender.
Remove the bay leaf. If a thick sauce is
desired, sprinkle with wholemeal flour
and cook for a further few minutes to
thicken.

3. Serve, if wished, with a dollop of
soured cream and sprinkle with chopped
chervil.

BAKED POTATO [S]
DUMPLINGS

1½lb (680g) potatoes
Sea salt and freshly ground black
pepper
1 egg yolk
2-3 oz (55-85g) wholemeal flour
2 oz (55g) butter

1. Cook the potatoes in their skins until
tender, then drain and peel.

2. Put the potatoes through a sieve or
mouli and place in a bowl. Season with
salt and pepper, mix in the egg yolk and
add enough flour to make a dough,
kneading the mixture well.

3. Preheat the oven to 400°F/200°C (Gas
Mark 6).

4. Break pieces off the dough and roll
into dumplings or small croquettes. Melt
the butter in an ovenproof dish, arrange
the dumplings in one layer and bake
until golden-brown on one side. Turn
and brown the other side. Serve hot.

Note: If you wish to serve these
dumplings with spinach or other
vegetables, you can season them with
nutmeg, thyme, marjoram or other
herbs.

POTATO GNOCCHI [S]

2 lb (900g) potatoes ('old' ones are
preferable)
1 egg yolk
6 oz (170g) wholemeal flour
2 oz (55g) butter, melted
Sea salt and freshly ground black
pepper to taste
Handful of chopped parsley to
garnish

1. Cook the potatoes in their skins until they are tender, but still firm. Drain and peel, then put through a sieve or mouli. Turn into a bowl, mix in the egg yolk, then work in the flour and knead to a firm dough.

2. Bring a large saucepan of lightly salted water to the boil.

3. Meanwhile, turn the dough out onto a board. Divide the dough into pieces and roll between well-floured hands to form cylinders about ½ inch (1.25cm) in diameter. With a sharp knife, cut into 1-inch (2.5cm) lengths and pinch the centre of each lightly between the index finger and thumb. Place on a lightly floured cloth, taking care that they do not touch each other.

4. Drop into the rapidly boiling water and cook until they rise to the surface. (You will probably have to do this in batches.) Remove with a slotted spoon and drain.

5. To serve, toss lightly in a warmed serving dish with the butter. Season with salt and pepper and garnish with chopped parsley.

POTATO PANCAKES WITH ONION [S]

2 lb (900g) potatoes
1 teaspoonful butter
1 medium-sized onion, finely chopped
2 tablespoonful wholemeal flour
Pinch of sea salt and freshly ground black pepper
2 egg yolks, beaten
1 tablespoonful finely chopped parsley
2 teaspoonsful corn oil
Extra corn oil for frying

1. Peel the potatoes and grate them into cold water (this prevents discoloration), then drain, wrap in a clean tea towel and press out the excess moisture. Turn into a bowl.

2. Meanwhile, melt the butter in a small saucepan, add the onion and cook until transparent. Mix into the potatoes with the flour, salt, pepper, egg yolks, parsley and 2 teaspoonsful corn oil.

3. Heat a thin film of corn oil in a large frying pan. Drop tablespoonsful of the potato mixture into the pan, press with a spatula to flatten and fry until golden on both sides.

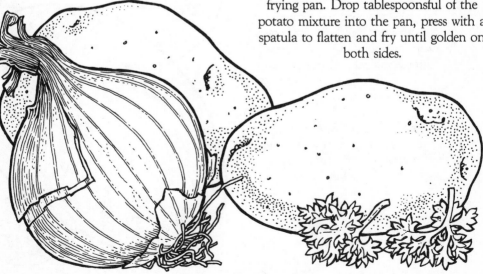

BAKED POTATO PURÉE [S]

**2 lb (900g) potatoes
Sea salt and freshly ground black
pepper to taste
2 tablespoonsful still mineral water
4 fl oz (120ml) soured cream
Butter
1 medium-sized onion, finely
chopped**

1. Cook the potatoes in their skins until tender. Drain and peel, then put through a sieve or mouli. Turn into a bowl and season with salt and pepper.

2. Heat the mineral water in a medium-sized saucepan over low heat. Stir in the soured cream. Tip in the potatoes, remove from the heat and beat with a wire whisk until light and fluffy.

3. Preheat the oven to 400°F/200°C (Gas Mark 6).

4. Grease an ovenproof dish with a little butter. Cover with an even layer of chopped onion. Heap on the potato purée and smooth the top, then make a pattern on the surface with the tines of a fork. Dot with butter and place the dish in the oven for about 15 minutes, until the butter is melted and the top is brown.

Variation:
Potato Purée with herbs. After you have puréed the potatoes, mix in a generous handful of chopped dillweed, chervil, parsley, basil or other herbs.

COUNTRY-STYLE POTATO CAKES [S]

**1 lb (450g) raw potatoes
3 cooked potatoes, roughly mashed
Pinch of sea salt, grated nutmeg and
freshly ground black pepper
Corn oil to grease**

1. Preheat the oven to 400°F/200°C (Gas Mark 6).

2. Grate the raw potatoes into a bowl. Mix in the cooked, mashed potatoes, salt, nutmeg and pepper.

3. Oil a baking sheet. Spoon little mounds of the potato mixture onto the baking sheet, then press them flat.

4. Bake in the oven for 20-30 minutes, turning the cakes over halfway through the baking time to brown both sides.

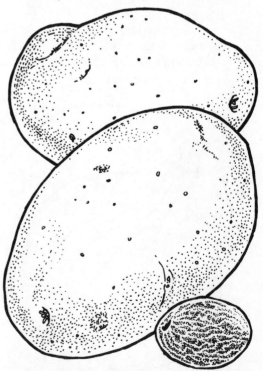

PASTA

In the following recipes, only wholewheat pasta should be used. This can now be bought in most supermarkets and health food shops, but make sure you buy the kind that is made without whole eggs.

However, nothing tastes as good as home-made pasta. A pasta machine is a very useful gadget since its different attachments automatically produce tagliatelle, spaghetti, macaroni and other shapes, but it is not difficult to make pasta by hand.

BASIC HOME-MADE $\boxed{S}$ PASTA

1 lb (450g) wholemeal bread flour
1 teaspoonful sea salt
4 large egg yolks
1 tablespoonful olive oil
3 tablespoonsful cold water
(approximately)

1. Sift the flour and salt into a large bowl. Make a well in the centre and tip the egg yolks into the well. Add the olive oil and water. With the fingers or a wooden spoon, gradually incorporate the flour into the liquid ingredients. Work the dough very thoroughly until it holds together in a stiff ball, adding a little more water if necessary. (The dough will soften after kneading and resting.)

2. Knead the dough well for about 15 minutes by hand or in an electric mixer fitted with a dough hook for about 5 minutes. (When there are little air bubbles beneath the surface of the dough, it is ready.)

3. Roll the dough into a ball, wrap loosely in a polythene bag and set aside for at least 1 hour to allow the dough to relax. (If you want to keep it overnight, store in the refrigerator without sealing the bag.)

4. Roll the dough out as thinly as possible on a lightly floured surface with a floured rolling pin, then cut into the desired shapes. Alternatively, put the dough through a pasta machine, following the manufacturer's recommendations.

5. Leave the pasta to dry for at least 1 hour, either on a floured tea towel, covered by another tea towel or draped over a clean broomstick handle supported by two chairs.

6. To cook, bring 6 pints (3.5 litres) of lightly salted water to the boil. Add the pasta and bring back to the boil. Home-made pasta cooks very quickly, so start testing almost immediately. Cook until just *al dente* — firm to the bite. Drain and use as desired.

Variations:

Green Pasta
Reduce the flour to ¾ lb (340g). Eliminate the egg yolks. Cook ½ lb (225g) fresh or frozen spinach, then purée until smooth. Place in the well with the other ingredients and proceed as in the previous recipe.

Herb Pasta
Add a handful of very finely chopped herbs of your choice to the basic recipe.

PASTA WITH TOASTED BREADCRUMBS [S]

8 fl oz (240ml) cold-pressed olive oil
4 cloves garlic, finely chopped
6 oz (170g) dry wholemeal
breadcrumbs
2 oz (55g) fresh parsley, chopped
Sea salt and freshly ground black
pepper to taste
1 recipe quantity Basic Home-made
Pasta (page 67)

1. Heat 1 tablespoonful of the oil in a
medium-sized frying pan. Add the garlic
and sauté until golden. Remove the garlic
from the pan with a slotted spoon and
set aside.

2. Add the remaining oil to the frying
pan. Stir in the breadcrumbs to coat
evenly. Toast over moderate heat, taking
care to see that the breadcrumbs do not
burn, stirring frequently until the
breadcrumbs are golden-brown. Remove
from the heat and mix in the garlic and
parsley. Season with salt and pepper.

3. Cook the pasta according to the
instructions on page 000. Drain and toss
with the breadcrumb mixture. Serve
immediately.

PASTA PRIMAVERA [S]

1 lb (450g) fresh seasonal vegetables,
cut into julienne strips and cooked
until crisply tender
Sea salt and freshly ground black
pepper to taste
1 recipe quantity Basic, Green or
Herb Pasta (page 67)

Sauce:
1 oz (30g) butter
2 tablespoonsful wholemeal flour
½ pint (300ml) Vegetable Stock
(page 37)

1. Place the vegetables in a bowl and
season with salt and pepper.

2. Make the sauce. Melt the butter in a
large saucepan, stir in the flour and cook
1 minute. Add the vegetable stock and
cook, stirring, until the sauce thickens.
Remove from the heat and mix in the
prepared vegetables. Keep warm while
cooking the pasta.

3. Cook the pasta in plenty of lightly
salted water until *al dente*. Drain and
toss with the vegetables and sauce. Turn
into a warmed serving dish and serve at
once.

PIQUANT PASTA BAKE [S]

7 oz (200g) wholewheat pasta
7 oz (200g) cream cheese *or* Quark
2 egg yolks
4 oz (115g) shallots, finely chopped
1 tablespoonful chopped sage
Sea salt and freshly ground black
pepper to taste
3 tablespoonsful soured cream
Butter

1. Cook the pasta in plenty of lightly salted water until *al dente*. Drain thoroughly.

2. Mix together in a bowl the cheese, egg yolks, shallots, sage, salt, pepper and soured cream.

3. Preheat the oven to 400°F/200°C (Gas Mark 6).

4. Grease an ovenproof dish with the butter, cover the base of the dish with a layer of pasta, then spread on a layer of the cheese mixture and continue until all the ingredients are used, ending with a thin layer of pasta. Dot with butter and bake in the oven for 20 minutes.

RICE

Use brown rice in the following recipes; it is much more nutritious than the white variety. It takes longer to cook, but has a lovely nutty taste.

If you mill your own flour at home, milling a little rice afterwards will clean your equipment. Brown rice flour may also be bought in health food shops. Rice flour can be used to thicken soups and sauces for starch meals.

BASIC BOILED RICE [S]

I cook rice by the volume method — 1 part rice to 2 parts water. Bring to the boil in a saucepan, then continue to cook either over very low heat, covered, or in a moderate oven 350°F/180°C (Gas Mark 4) also covered, for about 45 minutes, until the rice is tender and the water is absorbed. Fluff up with a fork. Soaking the rice before cooking will cut down on the cooking time.

CUCUMBER RICE [S]

½ lb (225g) long-grain brown rice, cooked
1 cucumber, diced
1 tablespoonful chopped dillweed
1 tablespoonful chopped borage
½ oz (15g) butter
Sea salt and freshly ground black
pepper to taste

1. Mix the hot cooked rice with the remaining ingredients, stirring until well-combined.

SERBIAN RICE [S]

2 tablespoonsful corn oil
2 large onions, finely chopped
3 leeks, trimmed and finely sliced
4 red peppers, deseeded and cut into
julienne strips
Sea salt and cayenne pepper to taste
1 pint (600ml) Vegetable Stock
(page 37)
5 oz (140g) long-grain brown rice
4 tomatoes, skinned and chopped

1. Heat the oil in a medium-sized saucepan. Add the onions and sauté until transparent. Add the leeks and peppers and season with salt and cayenne pepper.

2. Pour the vegetable stock into the saucepan. Add the rice and cook over low heat until tender. Remove from the heat.

3. Add the chopped tomatoes and serve at once. (Do not allow them to cook, or they will not be suitable for a starch meal.)

BUCKWHEAT

Buckwheat is a nutritious food that can be used in a variety of forms: the flakes can be made into muesli or used to thicken a sauce for vegetables; buckwheat flour can be substituted for wholemeal flour, or a combination of buckwheat and wholemeal flours can be used to make, for example, pasta. There are also many dishes that can be prepared using whole buckwheat.

BUCKWHEAT STUFFING [S]

½ oz (15g) butter
1 medium-sized onion, chopped
1 pint (600ml) Vegetable Stock
(page 37)
7 oz (200g) buckwheat
Sea salt and freshly ground black
pepper to taste
Chopped herbs

1. Melt the butter in a medium-sized saucepan over moderate heat. Add the onion and sauté until transparent.

2. Add the vegetable stock and bring to the boil. Reduce the heat to a simmer and add the buckwheat. Cook for about 20 minutes, until the buckwheat is tender, then remove from the heat and allow to cool.

3. Season to taste with salt and pepper and mix with chopped herbs of your choice.

4. Use to stuff cabbage leaves, peppers, aubergines or courgettes.

BUCKWHEAT DUMPLINGS [S]

7 oz (200g) soft wholemeal
breadcrumbs
7 oz (200g) buckwheat
Sea salt and freshly ground black
pepper
Handful of finely chopped parsley
2 egg yolks
1 tablespoonful cold-pressed olive oil
Few tablespoonsful hot still mineral
water

1. Mix all the ingredients together thoroughly, using only enough mineral water to make a firm dough. Allow to cool.

2. With wet hands, form the dough into dumplings. Bring a large saucepan of lightly salted water to the boil. Reduce the heat to a simmer and lower the dumplings gently into the water. Simmer for about 15 minutes.

3. Serve in soups and ragoûts or with a hot sauce.

SAVOURY BUCKWHEAT [S]

½ lb (225g) buckwheat
16 fl oz (480ml) lightly salted water
or Vegetable Stock (page 37)
2 cloves garlic, crushed
1 medium-sized onion, chopped
Handful of finely chopped parsley
½ oz (15g) butter

1. Preheat the oven to 350°F/180°C (Gas Mark 4).

2. Place the buckwheat and water or vegetable stock in a medium-sized saucepan and bring to the boil over moderate heat. Cover the pan, transfer to the oven and bake for 20 minutes, or until the liquid is absorbed.

3. Remove the saucepan from the oven and add the garlic, onion, parsley and butter. Fluff up with a fork and serve with a hot sauce or salad.

BUCKWHEAT PANCAKES [S]

10 oz (285g) buckwheat flour
1 oz (30g) fresh yeast
2 egg yolks
Pinch of sea salt
Few tablespoonsful soured cream
thinned with still mineral water
Butter or corn oil to fry
Savoury spread to serve (see pages 101-103)

1. Mix the buckwheat flour, yeast, egg yolks and salt with enough of the soured cream mixture to make a firm dough. Allow to rest for 30 minutes.

2. Melt the butter or heat the oil in a medium-sized frying pan over moderate heat. Divide the dough into small cakes, press to flatten into thin rounds and fry gently on both sides until golden brown. Keep the pancakes warm until the entire batch is cooked, then sandwich together with one of the savoury spreads on pages 101-103.

Variation:
These pancakes may also be served as a dessert for a **starch** meal. Add 1 teaspoonful fructose (fruit sugar) to the dough and substitute a fruit purée for the savoury spread.

MAIZE

Maize is another word for sweetcorn. When it is available fresh on the cob, you can cook it in plain boiling water. Some people add salt, but this tends to toughen the kernels. Cook only until the kernels are tender and serve with butter and a generous grinding of black pepper, or cut the kernels from the cob with a sharp knife, blanch and freeze them to use in salad and vegetable dishes in the winter months.

Cornflour and flakes are an alternative to wheat in many recipes. Maize grits, which may be obtained from some health food shops, also can be used to make delicious dishes.

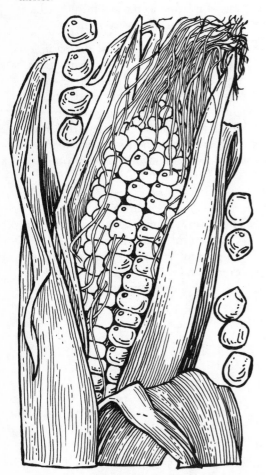

CORN-VEGETABLE BAKE [S]

1 oz (30g) butter
1 medium-sized onion, chopped
2 stalks celery, chopped
2 carrots, scraped and diced
2 parsnips, peeled and diced
1 small cauliflower, separated into florets
¾ lb (340g) maize grits
17 fl oz (500ml) Vegetable Stock (page 37)
Handful of finely chopped parsley
2 cloves garlic, finely chopped
1 tablespoonful finely chopped marjoram
Butter *or* soured cream to serve

1. Melt the butter in a medium-sized saucepan. Add the onion, celery, carrots, parsnips and cauliflower and sauté until vegetables are crisp-tender.

2. Preheat the oven to 350°F/180°F (Gas Mark 4). Grease an ovenproof casserole with a tight-fitting lid.

3. Turn the sautéed vegetables, maize grits, vegetable stock, parsley, garlic and marjoram into the casserole. Mix to combine and bake, covered until maize grits are tender and the liquid in the casserole has been absorbed. (If necessary, add a bit more vegetable stock.)

4. Serve hot, with a knob or two of butter or a dollop of soured cream.

MILLET

While millet is a staple grain in many tropical countries in Asia and Africa and has been cultivated for 6,000 years, in the West, it is primarily used for birdseed and feedstock. This is a pity, since it is very nutritious. It is high in proteins, carbohydrates and minerals. It is also very versatile — it can be used whole in many dishes; millet flakes can be used to thicken soups and sauces and millet flour can be used in baking (although not for leavened bread).

Since millet does not contain gluten, it is also a good choice for those on gluten-free diets. This mild-tasting, fragile grain can also be used to make porridge.

Millet is unique in being an alkaline-forming grain.

MILLET PORRIDGE   [S]

7 oz (200g) millet
16 fl oz (480ml) lightly salted water
Sliced bananas *or* other sweet fruit
to serve *or*
Sea salt, freshly ground black pepper
and a knob of butter

1. Rinse the millet in hot water, then drain.

2. Tip the millet into a medium-sized saucepan with the measured salted water and bring to the boil. Allow to boil for 3-4 minutes, then reduce the heat to very low and cook gently for about 15-20 minutes, until the water is absorbed.

3. Serve with sliced bananas or other sweet fruit or with a pinch of sea salt, a generous grinding of black pepper and a knob of butter.

MILLET WITH VEGETABLES   [S]

1 tablespoonful corn oil
1 medium-sized onion, finely chopped
1 green pepper, deseeded and cut into julienne strips
1 leek, trimmed and finely sliced
1 carrot, scraped and diced
1 small celeriac root, diced
Celeriac leaves, finely chopped
½ lb (225g) millet
1¼ pints (750ml) Vegetable Stock (page 37)
Knob of butter to serve

1. Heat the oil in a medium-sized saucepan. Add the onion and pepper and cook gently until softened. Add the leek, carrot, celeriac root and leaves and cook for a further few minutes.

2. Add the millet and vegetable stock to the pan. Bring to the boil, reduce the heat, cover and cook gently until the millet is tender.

3. Add a knob of butter and serve at once.

Note: If celeriac is unavailable, substitute another root vegetable of your choice.

MILLET CUTLETS ⬚S

14 oz (400g) millet
2 pints (1 litre) lightly salted water
1 tablespoonful cold-pressed olive oil
1 medium-sized onion, chopped
2 teaspoonsful soured cream
2 egg yolks
2 teaspoonsful millet flour or
wholemeal flour
Pinch of sea salt
1 clove garlic, crushed
Pinch of grated nutmeg
Corn oil to grease

1. Cook the millet in the water until the millet is tender and all the liquid has evoporated. Remove from the heat and set aside.

2. Heat the oil in a small frying pan and sauté the onion until transparent.

3. Add the onion to the millet along with the soured cream, egg yolks, millet flour or wholemeal flour, salt, garlic and nutmeg. Mix well and form into cutlets.

4. Preheat the oven to 400°F/200°C (Gas Mark 6). Brush a baking sheet with the corn coil.

5. Bake the cutlets until golden on both sides, turning them halfway through the baking time.

6. Serve with salad, vegetables or a hot sauce.

MUESLI

The following two recipes are ideas for basic mueslis. Add different fresh or dried *sweet* fruits for variety.

If you are constipated, the addition of a tablespoonful of bran to the muesli of your choice will help. (Bran is the husk of the grain which is sifted out of the flour used for baking.)

Muesli can be made with whole grains or flakes or a combination of both.

To aid the digestion, add ground linseeds or a little wheatgerm or sesame seed oil. Do not grind linseeds in a flour mill. They can be ground in a coffee grinder, but make sure you clean it thoroughly afterwards, as any residue left in the grinder will quickly go rancid.

These recipes are for single portions.

DR BIRCHER-BENNER'S MUESLI ⬚O

1 level tablespoon rolled oats or
medium oatmeal
3 tablespoonsful water
1 tablespoonful lemon juice
3 tablespoonsful raw milk if
obtainable or natural yogurt
7 oz (200g) apple (2 medium apples)
1 tablespoonful grated almonds or
hazelnuts

1. Soak the oats or oatmeal with the water overnight.

2. In the morning, add the lemon juice and grate the well-scrubbed apples into the mixture and sprinkle the grated nuts on top.

3. Serve at once.

Note: Reproduced from *Food Combining For Health* (Thorsons, 1984) by kind permission of the authors, Doris Grant and Jean Joice, who stress that this recipe is only neutral (alkaline) because of the *very* small quantity of cereal used.

OATFLAKE MUESLI ⑤

2 tablespoonful oatflakes
1 tablespoonful dried currants
1 tablespoonful chopped dried figs,
dates *or* prunes
2 teaspoonsful honey
Cream *or* milk to serve

1. Mix all the ingredients except for the milk or cream together.

2. Serve with just enough cream or milk to moisten the ingredients.

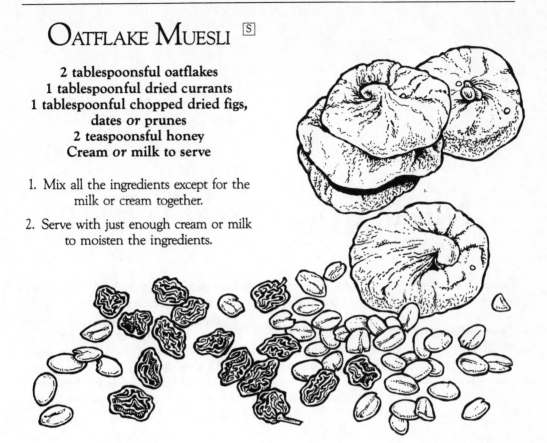

MEAT, POULTRY AND FISH

Those following the Hay System (or any other healthy diet) should eat very little meat — twice a week is plenty.

Fish and chicken are preferable to red meat. Avoid all forms of pork and any fatty meat.

Do not fry meat in breadcrumbs or in hot fat.

When buying meat, try to ensure that it has not been fattened artificially or fed hormones. Choose from beef, lamb, rabbit or hare, poultry (which should be free-range) and game.

If you can buy (or make) sausage meat that contains pure beef or chicken, all to the good, but it is difficult to find. Most sausages contain pork, bread and other ingredients that do not correspond with the requirements of this diet.

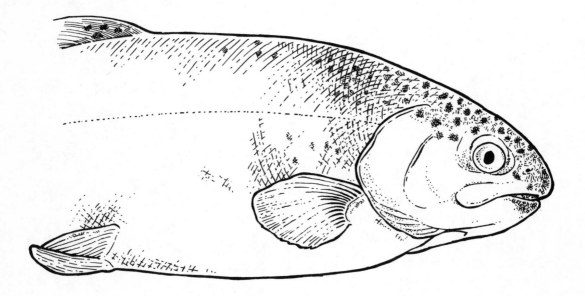

BEEF

AUSTRIAN BEEF IN CIDER P

½ pint (300ml) water
2 carrots, scraped and chopped
1 handful chopped parsley
2 stalks celery, chopped
2 leeks, trimmed and sliced
1 parsnip, peeled and chopped
1 onion, chopped
1 bay leaf
Few black peppercorns
Few juniper berries
1 pint (600ml) cider
2¼ lb (1kg) boned, rolled topside of beef
Sea salt
1 teaspoonful chopped marjoram
2 tablespoonsful Dijon mustard
½ oz (15g) butter
1 teaspoonful potato flour
¼ pint (140ml) soured cream
Few chopped prunes
Few walnut halves

1. First make the marinade. Pour the water into a medium-sized saucepan. Add the carrots, parsley, celery, leeks, parsnip, onion, bay leaf, peppercorns and juniper berries. Bring to the boil over moderate heat, then reduce the heat and simmer for 15 minutes. Remove the marinade from the heat and leave to cool, then stir in the cider. Place the beef in a flameproof casserole, pour over the cold marinade, cover the casserole and place in the refrigerator for 3 days. Each day, pour the marinade into a saucepan and bring it to the boil, then cool and pour over the meat.

2. On the third day, remove the beef from the casserole and allow to drain. Reserve the marinade. Rub the beef all over with a little salt and the marjoram. Spread with mustard.

3. Rinse and dry the casserole, add the butter and place over low heat. When the butter melts, add the beef and brown on all sides. Increase the heat, pour the marinade over and bring to the boil. Reduce the heat and simmer slowly for 1½-2 hours, until the beef is tender.

4. When the beef is done, remove it from the casserole onto a warmed serving dish. Stir the potato flour into the soured cream and add to the casserole with the prunes and walnuts. Heat through and serve immediately.

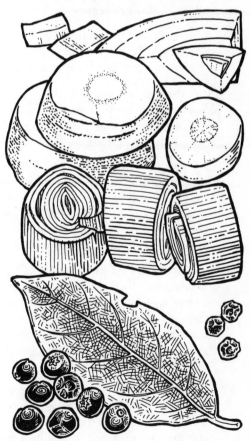

POT-ROASTED BEEF WITH JUNIPER [P]

2¼ lb (1kg) boned, rolled topside of
beef
1½ tablespoonsful crushed juniper
berries

Marinade:
1 pint (600ml) water
¼ pint (140ml) cider vinegar
1 onion, chopped
Rind of ½ lemon
1 teaspoonful juniper berries
Few sprigs rosemary
Pinch of sea salt
Few black peppercorns
Handful of chopped parsley
Celery leaves

½ oz (15g) butter
¼ pint (140ml) soured cream
Few crushed juniper berries to serve

1. Rub the joint of beef with the crushed
juniper berries. Wrap in aluminium foil
and store for at least 2 days in the
refrigerator.

2. Prepare the marinade. Mix all the
remaining ingredients except for the butter,
soured cream and crushed juniper berries
in a saucepan, bring to the boil, reduce
the heat and simmer for 15 minutes.
Remove from the heat and cool.

3. Place the beef in a flameproof
casserole, pour the cold marinade over,
cover the casserole and place back in the
refrigerator. Marinate for 3 days. Each
day, pour the marinade into a saucepan
and bring it to the boil, then cool and
pour over the meat.

4. On the third day, remove the meat
from the casserole and bring the
marinade to a boil. Pour off the
marinade into a jug, reduce the heat to

low and melt the butter in the casserole.
Brown the beef on all sides, add a little
of the marinade, cover and cook slowly
for 1½-2 hours, adding a little bit more
of the marinade to the casserole every so
often until the meat is tender.

5. When the beef is done, remove it
from the casserole onto a warmed serving
dish. Add any remaining marinade to
the casserole, stir in the soured cream
and heat through. Pour the sauce into a
sauceboat.

5. Just before serving, add a few crushed
juniper berries to the sauce.

CHICKEN

CHICKEN BREASTS WITH CHEESE [P]

4 boneless, skinless chicken breasts
Sea salt and freshly ground black
pepper
Soya flour to coat
1 oz (30g) butter
4 oz (115g) Emmental cheese, sliced
Grated Parmesan cheese
¼ pint (140ml) chicken stock

1. Preheat the oven to 350°F/180°C (Gas
Mark 4).

2. Pound the chicken breasts between
two sheets of greaseproof paper with a
meat mallet or rolling pin.

3. Sprinkle the chicken with salt and
pepper and coat lightly with soya flour.

4. Melt the butter in a frying pan large
enough to accomodate the chicken in
one layer and sauté for 5 minutes on
each side until golden-brown. Remove
from the heat and transfer to an

ovenproof dish. Lay the Emmental cheese slices over the chicken and sprinkle with grated Parmesan cheese. Pour over the chicken stock.

5. Bake, uncovered in the oven until the chicken is cooked, about 20 minutes.

CHICKEN BURGERS [P]

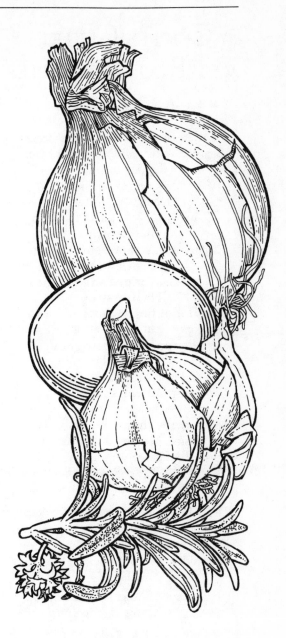

14 oz (400g) cooked chicken meat, minced
1 egg, beaten
1 tablespoonful corn oil
1 medium-sized onion, finely chopped
1 clove garlic, chopped
Handful of finely chopped parsley
1 teaspoonful chopped basil
1 teaspoonful chopped rosemary
Sea salt and freshly ground black pepper to taste
Corn oil to grease

1. Mix the minced chicken and egg.

2. Heat the oil in a small frying pan and sauté the onion until transparent. Add to the chicken mixture with the garlic, parsley, basil, rosemary, salt and pepper.

3. Preheat the oven to 350°F/180°C (Gas Mark 4). Brush a baking sheet with the corn oil. Form the chicken mixture into burgers and bake in the oven until both sides are golden-brown, turning the burgers halfway through the baking time.

CHICKEN CUTLETS [P] WITH ROOT VEGETABLES AND HERBS

4 boneless, skinless chicken breasts
Sea salt and freshly ground black
pepper to taste
Soya flour to coat
1 oz (30g) butter
2 turnips, peeled and cut into
julienne strips
2 parsnips, scraped and cut into
julienne strips
2 carrots, scraped and cut into
julienne strips
Handful of finely chopped parsley
1 tablespoonful finely chopped sorrel
1 tablespoonful finely chopped
chervil
Dash of lemon juice
½ pint (300ml) soured cream

1. Pound the chicken breasts as flat as possible between two sheets of greaseproof paper with a meat mallet. Season with salt and pepper and dust with soya flour.

2. Melt half of the butter in a frying pan large enough to accomodate the chicken in one layer and sauté on both sides until golden. Remove from the heat and set aside.

3. Melt the remaining butter in a large saucepan. Add the turnips, parsnips, carrots, parsley, sorrel and chervil. Pour in a little water and cook for a few minutes, then add the chicken, lemon juice and chicken stock and cook slowly for about 30 minutes, until the chicken and vegetables are tender. Remove the chicken to a warmed serving dish with a slotted spoon and keep warm.

4. Pour the stock and vegetables from the saucepan into a blender container and purée, adding a little extra water if necessary. Finally, stir in the soured cream, heat through and serve immediately with the chicken.

GARLIC-ROSEMARY [P] CHICKEN

2 large chicken breasts
Sea salt and freshly ground black
pepper
Soya flour to coat
3 oz (85g) butter
2 cloves garlic, crushed
1 teaspoonful chopped rosemary
¼ pint (140ml) single cream
1 teaspoonful cayenne pepper
Parsley sprigs and lemon wedges to
garnish

1. With a very sharp knife, cut the chicken breasts into thin slices. (Reserve the bones for stock.) Sprinkle with salt and pepper and coat lightly with soya flour.

2. Melt 1 oz (30g) of the butter in a large frying pan. Sauté the chicken and garlic until tender, sprinkle with rosemary and remove the chicken to a warmed serving dish with a slotted spoon.

3. Stir the cream, cayenne pepper and remaining butter into the pan, scraping the bottom of the pan with a wooden spoon. When the sauce is hot, return the chicken to the pan for a minute or two, then transfer to the serving dish.

4. Garnish with sprigs of parsley and lemon wedges.

Paprika Chicken [P]

1 oz (30g) butter
1 lb (450g) onions, chopped
1 chicken, jointed (see note below)
Sea salt to taste
1 tablespoonful paprika
Chicken stock
½ tablespoonful potato flour
¼ pint (140ml) soured cream

1. Melt the butter in a flameproof casserole over moderate heat. Add the onions and garlic and sauté until translucent.

2. Add the chicken to the pan and sprinkle lightly with salt. Dust with paprika and pour over enough chicken stock to cover the chicken. Bring to the boil, reduce the heat and simmer gently until the chicken is tender.

3. Remove the chicken from the pan onto a warmed serving dish. Increase the heat to reduce the stock. Remove the skin from the chicken and discard.

4. Meanwhile, mix the potato flour with a little water into a paste and add to the stock. Cook for a minute or two, then add the soured cream, mix well and remove from the heat.

5. Pour a little of the sauce over the chicken and pass the rest separately.

Note: You may use a boiling fowl for this dish, but it should be cooked first in a pressure cooker.

Spiced Chicken [P]

½ oz (15g) butter
1 medium-sized onion, chopped
2 cloves garlic, chopped
1 tart apple, chopped
2 teaspoonsful curry powder
2 teaspoonsful cayenne pepper
Pinch of grated nutmeg
2 large tomatoes, skinned and chopped
1 pint (600ml) water
Dash of cider vinegar
Few drops of soy sauce
1 chicken, 2½-3lb (1.2-1.5kg), cut into 8 pieces
4 oz (115g) almonds, chopped
Gherkins or mixed pickles to garnish

1. Melt the butter in a flameproof casserole and sauté the onion, garlic and apple lightly.

2. Stir in the curry powder, cayenne pepper and nutmeg and cook briefly, then add the tomatoes, water, vinegar, soy sauce and chicken. Bring to the boil, reduce the heat, cover and cook gently for about 30 minutes, until the chicken is tender.

3. Just before the end of the cooking time, stir in the almonds.

4. Serve garnished with gherkins or mixed pickles.

STUFFED CHICKEN P
BAKED IN A BRICK

Stuffing:
½ lb (225g) minced chicken
Pinch of sea salt
Few green peppercorns
1 teaspoonful chopped basil
Pinch of grated nutmeg
½ teaspoonful chopped marjoram
1 tablespoonful chopped parsley
½ teaspoonful chopped rosemary
1 medium-sized cooked onion, sliced

1 whole chicken, about 3 lb (1.5kg)
Sea salt, paprika and rosemary,
mixed
2 carrots, scraped and coarsely
chopped
2 stalks celery, chopped
1 onion, chopped
Few cloves garlic, crushed
White wine

1. First prepare the chicken brick by soaking it in water for 20 minutes.

2. Meanwhile, prepare the stuffing. Mix together the minced chicken, salt, green peppercorns, basil, nutmeg, marjoram, parsley, rosemary and sliced onion. When the stuffing is well-combined, stuff the chicken and skewer or sew the opening together. Rub the chicken skin with a mixture of salt, paprika and rosemary.

3. Preheat the oven to 350°F/180°C (Gas Mark 4).

4. Place the chicken in the brick and surround it with the carrots, celery, onion and garlic. Pour in the white wine to a depth of about 1 inch (2.5cm). Place the lid on the brick and bake for 1-1½ hours.

MINCED MEAT
CURRIED MEAT P
LOAF

14 oz (400g) minced beef
1 medium-sized onion, finely
chopped
1 egg, beaten
¼ teaspoonful freshly ground black
pepper
½-1 tablespoonful curry powder
Sea salt to taste
2 tablespoonsful finely chopped
parsley
Soya flour
Butter to grease
¼ pint (140ml) Vegetable Stock (page
37)
Soured cream (optional)

1. Mix together in a bowl the minced beef, onion, egg, pepper, curry powder, salt and parsley.

2. Sprinkle a little soya flour on a pastry board and form the mixture into a loaf.

3. Preheat the oven to 350°F/180°C (Gas Mark 4). Grease an ovenproof dish with the butter and place the meat loaf inside. Pour over the vegetable stock and bake in the oven for about 30-45 minutes.

4. Stir a few spoonsful of soured cream into the meat juices before serving, if desired.

LINZ CABBAGE AND BEEF BAKE ⓟ

½ oz (15g) butter
1 medium-sized onion, roughly chopped
½ lb (225g) minced beef (*or* lamb or chicken)
2 green peppers, deseeded and chopped
Pinch of paprika
2 cloves garlic, crushed
1 small cabbage, coarsely shredded
Pinch of cayenne pepper
½ pint (300ml) Vegetable Stock (page 37)
Few drops soy sauce
1 tablespoonful finely chopped parsley
1 tablespoonful finely chopped celery leaves
Butter to grease
1 egg
¼ pint (140ml) soured cream

1. Melt the butter in a large frying pan and sauté the onion until transparent. Add the minced meat, green peppers, paprika, sea salt and garlic and cook, stirring, until the meat has coloured.

2. Add the cabbage, cayenne pepper, vegetable stock and soy sauce. Sprinkle with the parsley and celery leaves and continue to cook until all the liquid has evaporated. Remove from the heat.

3. Preheat the oven to 350°F/180°C (Gas Mark 4).

4. Grease a 1 lb (450g) loaf tin or oval ovenproof dish with the butter. Turn the meat mixture into the tin.

5. Whisk together the egg and soured cream in a cup and pour over the meat.

6. Bake in the oven for about 30 minutes.

STUFFED PEPPERS ⓟ

4 green peppers
½ lb (225g) minced beef
Handful of finely chopped parsley
1 small onion, finely chopped
3 cloves garlic, finely chopped
½ teaspoonful paprika
1 teaspoonful chopped marjoram
1 egg yolk
Sea salt to taste
¾ lb (340g) tomatoes, skinned and chopped
1 oz (30g) butter

1. Slice the tops off the peppers; scrape out the pith and seeds and set the peppers aside.

2. Mix together the minced beef, parsley, onion, garlic, paprika, marjoram, egg yolk and salt in a bowl. Stuff the peppers with this mixture.

3. Purée the tomatoes in a blender with a little water. Pour the tomato purée into a shallow flameproof pan, arrange the stuffed peppers upright in the pan and place over low heat. Cook gently until done.

4. Serve hot, topped with butter.

LAMB

LAMB GOULASH [P]

1 oz (30g) butter
1 lb (450g) onions, sliced
1 green pepper, deseeded and cut
into julienne strips
3 lb (1.4kg) shoulder of lamb, boned
and cut into 1-inch (2.5cm) cubes
Sea salt and freshly ground black
pepper
1 tablespoonful finely chopped chilli
peppers
Few sage leaves
Generous pinch of paprika

1. Melt the butter in a flameproof casserole. Add the onions and green pepper and sauté until the vegetables are softened. Remove the vegetables with a slotted spoon and set aside.

2. Preheat the oven to 350°F/180°C (Gas Mark 4).

3. Add the lamb to the casserole, sprinkle lightly with salt and pepper and sauté lightly. Remove from the heat, return the onions and green pepper to the pan along with the chillies, sage and paprika.

4. Cover the casserole and bake in the oven for about 2 hours, until the lamb is very tender.

5. Serve the lamb with the vegetables and pan juices.

OVEN-STEAMED SADDLE OF LAMB [P]

For this recipe, it is best to buy a six-month old lamb, weighing 3½-4 lb (1.5-2kg). Ask the butcher to bone it for you so that you can roll up the saddle. Also ask for the bones to make stock. It is best to give the butcher plenty of notice.

1 spring lamb 3½-4lb (1½-2 kg)
Sea salt
2 cloves garlic, crushed
Water
Lamb bones
Fresh *or* dried sage
Broccoli and cauliflower florets, baby
carrots, radish roses and parsley to
garnish

1. Preheat the oven to 350°F/180°C (Gas Mark 4).

2. Rub the lamb all over with sea salt and crushed garlic, then roll up and tie at intervals with kitchen string.

3. Place the meat in a lidded roasting tin with a little water, the bones and a few fresh or dried sage leaves. Cover the tin tightly with a lid and cook for about 1½ hours. (The lamb should steam, rather than roast.) Check frequently to make sure there is water in the tin. Fifteen minutes before serving, remove the foil to allow the meat to brown.

4. When the lamb is done, bring it whole to the table on a large meat platter. Garnish with broccoli, cauliflower, carrots, radish roses and parsley. Carve at the table.

RABBIT AND HARE

JUGGED HARE $\boxed{P}$

Marinade:
1 stalk celery, chopped
1 carrot, scraped and chopped
1 celeriac root, chopped
1 leek, trimmed and sliced
1 bay leaf
Few black peppercorns
Few juniper berries
1 clove garlic, crushed
1 onion, sliced
1 pint (600ml) lightly salted water
1 young hare, about 3½ lb (1.5kg)
Few tablespoonsful soured cream
Dash of white wine
Potato flour to thicken sauce
(optional)

1. First make the marinade. Place the celery, carrot, parsley root, leek, bay leaf, peppercorns, juniper berries, garlic and onion in a medium-sized saucepan. Add the water, bring to the boil and simmer for 1 hour. Cook, then pour the marinade over the hare and let it stand for a few days. (If the hare is very young, the standing period can be reduced to a few hours.)

2. Preheat the oven to 325°F/170°C (Gas Mark 3).

3. Transfer the hare to an ovenproof casserole. Strain a little of the marinade and pour over the hare. Cover the casserole tightly with a lid and cook gently for about 3 hours, until the hare is very tender.

4. A few minutes before serving, make a sauce by simmering the remaining marinade to reduce it. Stir in a few tablespoonsful soured cream and a dash

of white wine plus the potato flour, if using. Remove from the heat.

Note: If celeriac is unavailable, substitute another root vegetable of your choice.

RABBIT-IN-A-POT $\boxed{P}$

2¼ lb (1kg) rabbit portions
Sea salt
Water *or* chicken stock
1 teaspoonful chopped sage *or* wild thyme
2 cloves garlic, crushed
1 teaspoonful chopped lovage
Potato flour and soured cream to thicken sauce (optional)

1. Preheat the oven to 325°F/170°C (Gas Mark 3).

2. Sprinkle the rabbit portions with salt and place in an ovenproof casserole with the water or chicken stock, sage or wild thyme, garlic and lovage. Bake for about 1½ hours, or until tender.

3. Serve as is or thicken the cooking juices with a little potato flour and a few spoonsful of soured cream to make a sauce.

RABBIT STEW [P]

1 oz (30g) butter
2¼ lb (1kg) cubed rabbit
1 onion, chopped
1 carrot, scraped and diced
1 celeriac root, chopped
1 leek, thinly sliced
2 stalks celery, sliced
¾ pint (450ml) chicken stock
1 teaspoonful chopped sage
Few green peppercorns
1 teaspoonful chopped lovage
4 tablespoonsful soured cream
Potato flour to thicken sauce
(optional)
Few gherkins, chopped

1. Melt the butter in a large flameproof casserole. Brown the rabbit lightly, then remove from the pan with a slotted spoon and set aside. Add the onion, carrot, celeriac root, leek and celery to the casserole and cook until softened.

2. Return the rabbit to the casserole and pour over the chicken stock. Add the sage, green peppercorns and lovage. Bring to the boil, reduce the heat and simmer gently for about an hour, until the rabbit is tender.

3. Stir the soured cream into the sauce and thicken with potato flour if desired. Just before serving, add the chopped gherkins.

Note: If celeriac is unavailable, substitute another root vegetable of your choice.

FISH

Fish is very nutritious. It is an excellent source of protein and is low in fat and carbohydrates. Choose non-oily varieties, which have a more delicate flavour and few calories.

Fish should not be deep-fried in batter. It should be poached, steamed or baked.

The best method of cooking fish is to poach it. Poached fish is most easily digested. A good investment is a fish poacher — no other method leaves fish so moist or pure in flavour. Fish needs only a very short poaching time, but it should be handled carefully to ensure that it remains whole. Do not allow the water to boil, and wrap the fish in a double layer of muslin so that you can lift it safely from the poaching rack.

CURRIED SEA BASS [P]

Whole sea bass, approximately 3 lb
(1.5kg), cleaned
Juice of 1 lemon
2 onions, chopped
½ oz (15g) butter
2 tart apples, sliced
Few green peppercorns
Sea salt
Curry powder to taste
Dash of dry white wine
Lemon slices, sprigs of parsley and
cooked apple rings to garnish

1. Preheat the oven to 350°F/180°C (Gas Mark 4).

2. Rinse the fish, dry with absorbent kitchen paper, sprinkle with lemon juice and set aside.

3. Melt the butter in a flameproof casserole and sauté the onions until transparent. Remove from the heat. Add the apples and peppercorns to the casserole and place the fish on top.

Sprinkle with a little sea salt and curry powder, add a dash of dry white wine and cover the casserole tightly with aluminium foil.

4. Bake in the oven for about 25-30 minutes, until the fish flakes easily with a fork and the flesh is opaque. Do not overcook.

5. Garnish with lemon, parsley and apple rings.

MEXICAN CEVICHE P

1 lb (450g) white fish fillets, skinned and cut into thin strips
1 teaspoonful coriander seeds
1 teaspoonful black peppercorns
Juice of 6 limes
1 teaspoonful sea salt
Tomato wedges and lime slices to serve

1. Place the fish in a bowl.

2. With a pestle and mortar, reduce the coriander seeds and peppercorns to a fine powder.

3. In another bowl, mix the lime juice, sea salt and crushed sprices. Pour over the fish. Cover and chill in the refrigerator for 24 hours, turning the fish occasionally. .

4. Serve with tomato wedges and lime slices.

Note: The acidity of the lime juice 'cooks' the fish in this recipe.

HUNGARIAN COD P
CUTLETS

4 cod cutlets
Juice and rind of 1 lemon
2 oz (55g) butter
Pinch of sea salt
2 tablespoonsful chopped parsley
1 red pepper, deseeded and cut into julienne strips
1 green pepper, deseeded and cut into julienne strips
1 yellow pepper, deseeded and cut into julienne strips
1 onion, sliced
2 courgettes, sliced
Paprika
2 tomatoes, sliced to garnish

1. Pat the cod cutlets dry with absorbent kitchen paper and sprinkle with the lemon juice. Set the fish aside for 15 minutes.

2. Meanwhile, preheat the oven to 350°F/180°C (Gas Mark 4).

3. Melt half the butter in an ovenproof dish in the oven. Place the fish cutlets in the dish with a pinch of salt and sprinkle with parsley.

4. Cut the lemon rind into thin strips and scatter over the fish. Bake in the oven for 20 minutes, or until the fish flakes easily with a fork.

5. Meanwhile, melt the remaining butter in a frying pan and sauté the onion and courgettes until tender. Sprinkle with paprika.

6. Serve the fish with the sautéed vegetables and garnish with sliced tomatoes.

FISHERMAN'S STEW [P]

2 tablespoonsful cold-pressed olive
oil
2 medium-sized onions, finely
chopped
Pinch of cayenne pepper
2 red peppers, deseeded and cut into
julienne strips
2 green peppers, deseeded and cut
into julienne strips
2 yellow peppers, deseeded and cut
into julienne strips
1 teaspoonful very finely chopped
chilli peppers
Pinch of thyme
Potato flour (optional)
½ pint (300ml) single cream
½ pint (300ml) Fish Stock (page 41)
or water
Juice of 1 lemon
2¼ lb (1kg) haddock fillets, skinned
and cut into cubes
Chopped parsley to garnish

1. Heat the oil in a flameproof casserole
over moderate heat. Sauté the onions
until transparent. Add the cayenne
pepper and red, green and yellow
peppers. Stir. Add the chillies and
thyme. Sprinkle with potato flour if you
prefer a thicker sauce, then stir in the
cream, fish stock or water and lemon
juice. Cook for a few minutes, until the
sauce is barely simmering.

2. Add the fish and stir once. Cover the
casserole and cook slowly until the fish is
done, about 10-15 minutes. Garnish with
parsley and serve.

CHEESY FISH FILLETS [P]

4 white fish fillets, skinned
Sea salt
Lemon juice
1 oz (30g) butter
2 tablespoonsful finely chopped
onion
2 teaspoonsful chopped sage
4 slices Cheddar cheese
Sautéed tomatoes to garnish

1. Preheat the oven to 350°F/180°C (Gas
Mark 4).

2. Sprinkle the fish fillets with salt and
lemon juice and place in a greased
ovenproof dish that will just accomodate
them. Sprinkle with onion and sage and
bake for about 10 minutes. Arrange a
slice of cheese over each fillet, dot with
butter and continue baking for another
10 minutes, until the cheese is melted
and the fish flakes easily with a fork.

3. Garnish with sautéed tomatoes.

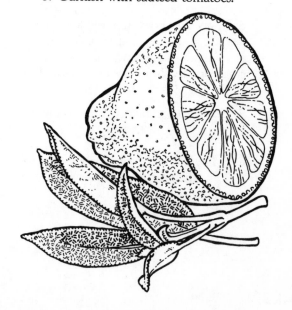

Fish with Chilli [P]

½ oz (15g) butter
2 onions, chopped
2 cloves garlic, crushed
1 teaspoonful cumin seeds
1 chilli pepper, very finely chopped
2 lb (900g) fish fillets, skinned
½ pint (300ml) Fish Stock (page 41)
½ tablespoonful potato flour
1 large carrot, scraped, diced and
lightly steamed
1-2 courgettes, diced and lightly
steamed
4 oz (115g) fresh or frozen peas,
lightly cooked
1 oz (30g) butter
Finely chopped parsley to garnish

1. Melt the butter in a medium-sized saucepan over moderate heat and sauté the onions until transparent. Add the garlic, cumin seeds and chilli pepper and sauté briefly. Remove from the heat.

2. Cut the fish fillets into strips, taking care to see that all the bones have been removed and mix together with the onion mixture in an ovenproof dish.

3. Preheat the oven to 350°F/180°C (Gas Mark 4).

4. Pour the fish stock into a saucepan and place over moderate heat. Stir in the potato flour mixed with a little of the stock to a paste and cook until it thickens. Pour the sauce over the fish. Arrange little mounds of carrots, courgettes and peas around the fish, dot with butter and bake in the oven for 15-20 minutes, until the fish is cooked.

5. Serve sprinkled with finely chopped parsley.

Baked Herrings with Herbs [P]

8 fresh herrings, cleaned
Sea salt
Butter to grease
1 bay leaf
Sprig of thyme
Sprigs of chervil and lemon wedges
to garnish
Sautéed tomato halves to serve

1. Preheat the oven to 350°F/180°C (Gas Mark 4).

2. Wash the herrings well, inside and out and dry with absorbent kitchen paper. Rub the flesh with salt.

3. Grease an oblong, lidded ovenproof dish with the butter and fit the herrings in snugly, placing them alternately head to tail. Tuck in a bay leaf and sprig of thyme, cover the dish and bake in the oven for about 30 minutes, until the fish are firm.

4. Remove from the oven and tuck a sprig of chervil in the herrings' mouths. Garnish with lemon wedges. Serve directly from the baking dish with sautéed tomato halves.

PAUPIETTES OF PERCH [P]

8 perch fillets, skinned
Pinch of sea salt
1 egg
Bunch of dillweed, chopped
Few green peppercorns
Juice of 1 lemon
1 onion, chopped
1 small chilli pepper, seeded and
chopped
¼ pint (140ml) water
¼ pint (140ml) soured cream
1 tablespoonful chopped parsley
1 egg yolk

1. Cut the ends off the fish fillets to
make neat rectangles. Place the
trimmings that you have cut off in a
blender or food processor with a pinch
of salt and the egg and blend to a purée.
Stir in the dillweed and peppercorns.

2. Salt the fillets lightly, sprinkle with
some of the lemon juice and spread
thinly with the purée. Roll up and secure
with thread.

3. Place the onion, chilli, water and
remainder of the lemon juice in a large
saucepan. Arrange the fish rolls on top
and cook over gentle heat for about 15
minutes, until the fish is cooked.

4. Remove the fish rolls carefully from
the pan, arrange on a serving dish and
keep warm.

5. Stir the soured cream and parsley into
the pan, allow to cook briefly, then
remove from the heat and whisk in the
egg yolk. Pour the sauce over the
paupiettes.

STUFFED SNAPPER IN WINE SAUCE [P]

1 red snapper, 3-lb (1.5kg), or other
whole white fish, cleaned
Sea salt
Juice of 1 lemon
1 green pepper, deseeded and
chopped
Handful of parsley, chopped
¼ pint (140ml) Fish Stock (page 41)
¼ pint (140ml) dry white wine
2 tablespoonsful chopped lemon
balm
1 oz (30g) butter
Lemon slices to garnish
Cherry tomatoes to garnish

1. Rinse the fish inside and out and pat
dry with absorbent kitchen paper.
Sprinkle inside and out with salt and
lemon juice.

2. Preheat the oven to 350°F/180°C (Gas
Mark 4).

3. Stuff the fish with the green pepper
and parsley and place in a lidded
ovenproof dish.

4. Heat the fish stock with the wine and
pour around the fish. Sprinkle with
lemon balm, dot with butter and cover
the dish. Bake for 30-40 minutes or until
the fish flakes easily with a fork.

5. Serve garnished with lemon slices and
cherry tomatoes.

STEAMED SOLE WITH [P] CREAM SAUCE

Butter to grease
4 fillets of sole *or* plaice
Sea salt and freshly ground pepper
to taste

Sauce:
¼ pint (140ml) dry white wine
¼ pint (140ml) soured cream
Handful of chopped parsley
1 egg yolk
Sea salt and freshly ground black
pepper
Lemon wedges and sprigs of parsley
to garnish

1. Choose a saucepan that is only slightly smaller in diameter than a dinner plate, fill with water, bring to the boil and reduce the heat to a simmer.

2. Grease two dinner plates with the butter. Place the fish fillets between the two plates and arrange over the saucepan. Steam for 10-15 minutes, or until the fish flakes with a fork and is firm to the touch.

3. Meanwhile, prepare the sauce. Pour the wine into a small saucepan and place over moderate heat. Stir in the soured cream and parsley. Do not allow the sauce to boil. When it is hot, remove from the heat and whisk a little of the hot sauce into the egg yolk, then whisk the egg yolk mixture back into the sauce. Season with salt and pepper and keep warm.

4. To serve, pour the sauce over the fish and garnish with lemon and parsley.

MARINATED [P] BAKED TROUT

4 rainbow trout, approximately 7 oz
(200g) each, cleaned
2 oz (55g) butter
4 tablespoonsful lemon juice
Generous handful chopped parsley
1 clove garlic, finely chopped
Sea salt and freshly ground black
pepper
Sprigs of parsley to garnish

1. Rinse the trout and dry well with absorbent kitchen paper. Cut 3-4 diagonal slashes about ¼ inch (.5cm) deep on both sides of each trout. Place the fish in a shallow, lidded ovenproof dish.

2. Melt the butter in a small saucepan over low heat. Do not allow it to brown. When it has melted, remove from the heat and allow to cool. Mix in the lemon juice, parsley and garlic and pour over the fish.

3. Cover the dish tightly with cling film and set aside in a cool place for about 2 hours. After 1 hour, turn the fish around and baste with the marinade.

4. Preheat the oven to 350°F/180°C (Gas Mark 4). Remove the cling film and replace with aluminium foil. Bake in the oven for about 30-40 minutes, until the fish is firm to the touch and flakes easily with a fork.

5. Remove the foil and garnish with sprigs of parsley.

POACHED TROUT WITH BASIL SAUCE [P]

Court Bouillon:
1¼ pints (750ml) dry white wine
2 pints (1.1 litres) still mineral water
2 oz (55g) carrots, scraped and chopped
1 teaspoonful sea salt
Handful of chopped parsley
2 stalks celery, chopped
1 leek, trimmed and sliced
1 bay leaf
Pinch of thyme
Few green peppercorns
2 whole cloves
1 lemon, sliced
4 rainbow trout, approximately 7 oz (200g) each, cleaned

Sauce:
1½ tablespoonsful cold-pressed olive oil
1 oz (30g) basil, finely chopped
Juice of 1 lemon
Lemon slices and sprigs of parsley to garnish

1. First prepare the court bouillon. Place the ingredients in a fish poacher and bring to the boil. Meanwhile, wrap the fish in a double thickness of muslin and place on the poaching rack.

2. When the court bouillon is boiling, reduce the heat, lower the poaching rack into the pan, cover and barely simmer for 15 minutes. Meanwhile, prepare the sauce by mixing the oil, basil and lemon juice together in a cup.

3. Remove the fish from the pan, unwrap and place on a warmed serving plate. Pour the sauce over and garnish with lemon and parsley.

Variations:
Plain Poached Fish
Omit the olive oil, basil and lemon juice. Follow the above method for poaching any whole white fish. (Allow about ½ lb/225g) per person.) Serve the poaching liquid as a soup if desired, or thicken with soured cream, season to taste and sprinkle with fresh chopped herbs for a sauce. The court bouillon can also be frozen and re-used.

WHITING WITH HERBS [P]

4 whiting, cleaned
Sea salt
1 oz (30g) butter
1 tablespoonful chopped lemon balm
1 tablespoonful chopped mint
1 tablespoonful chopped chervil
1 tablespoonful chopped parsley
4 tomatoes, skinned and chopped
Soured cream to serve

1. Rinse the whiting and dry well with absorbent kitchen paper. Cut 3-4 diagonal slashes about ¼ inch (.5cm) deep on both sides of each whiting. Sprinkle with a little salt.

2. Melt the butter in a large frying pan over low heat. Add the fish to the pan and sauté slowly on both sides. When the fish are done, transfer carefully with a fish slice to a serving plate and keep warm.

3. Add the lemon balm, mint, chervil, parsley and tomatoes to the frying pan and stir to heat through briefly. Remove from the heat, pour over the fish and serve each fish with a dollop of soured cream.

SAUCES AND DRESSINGS

Sauces and dressings add interest to otherwise plain food.

They will perk up salads, vegetables, meat and poultry and even desserts. One thing to remember when making a sauce is that its flavour should complement, not mask the dish it is being served with. Using these recipes as a guide, it is possible to create many other sauces and dressings using different flavourings.

COLD SAUCES

HOME-MADE MAYONNAISE O P

2 egg yolks
Pinch of sea salt
Pinch of mustard powder
1 teaspoonful finely grated lemon rind*
¼ pint (140ml) cold-pressed olive oil

1. Whisk the egg yolks with the salt, mustard powder and lemon rind.

2. Add the oil, drop by drop, whisking after each addition. (This mayonnaise may also be made in a blender.) Chill in the refrigerator until needed or serve at room temperature.

Note: For a **protein** meal, you can use a whole egg, lemon juice to taste and a little more oil.

*From lemon guaranteed unsprayed with fungicide.

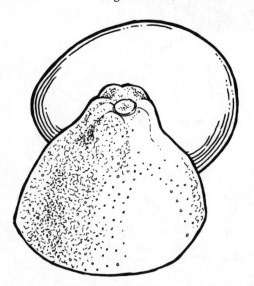

APPLE SAUCE P

1 lb (450g) apples, peeled, cored and quartered
Half a lemon, rind removed
Pinch of cinnamon

1. Place the apples in a medium-sized saucepan over low heat. Add the lemon and cinnamon and cook gently until soft. Remove from the heat.

2. Whisk until light and frothy or purée in a blender. Cook or chill in the refrigerator.

Note: This sauce can also be served hot with lamb.

AVOCADO SAUCE P

1 very ripe avocado
2 teaspoonsful cider vinegar
Pinch of mustard powder
1 tablespoonful finely chopped parsley *or* chives
1 clove garlic, crushed
Few shallots, chopped
1½ tablespoonsful cold-pressed olive oil

1. Cut the avocado in half, remove the stone and scrape the flesh from the skin into a bowl.

2. Mash the avodaco flesh until quite smooth, then stir in the vinegar, mustard powder, parsley or chives, garlic, shallots and oil.

COLD CAPER SAUCE ▢O

**4 tablespoonsful Home-made
Mayonnaise (page 94)
4 tablespoonsful yogurt
2 teaspoonsful finely chopped onion
Pinch of mustard powder
1 tablespoonful finely chopped
capers
Few whole capers to garnish**

1. Mix together the mayonnaise and yogurt in a cup.

2. Add the yogurt, onion, mustard powder and chopped capers. Stir well.

3. Garnish with a few whole capers.

GARLIC CREAM SAUCE ▢O

**½ pint (300ml) soured cream
3-4 cloves garlic, crushed
Sea salt and freshly ground pepper
to taste
3 tablespoonsful Home-Made
Mayonnaise (page 94)**

1. Mix together all the ingredients and chill in the refrigerator.

Note: For a protein meal, you can also add a dash of lemon juice.

HERB SAUCE ▢O▢S

**½ pint (300ml) natural yogurt
2 tablespoonsful Home-made
Mayonnaise (page 94)
Sea salt to taste
Handful of chopped seasonal herbs
Few drops soy sauce**

1. Pour the yogurt into a bowl and mix with the remaining ingredients.

2. Chill in the refrigerator until needed.

Variation:
For **starch** meals, substitute soured cream for the yogurt. Proceed as above.

GARLIC MAYONNAISE ▢P

**6 large cloves garlic, crushed
Sea salt to taste
2 egg yolks
1 tablespoonful finely chopped *or*
ground walnuts
¼ pint (140ml) cold-pressed olive oil
Juice of ½ lemon**

1. Crush the garlic with the salt to a pulp. Beat in the egg yolks and whisk until frothy. Stir in the walnuts.

2. Add the oil, one drop at a time and whisk after each addition.

3. When the mayonnaise is thick, whisk in the lemon juice and parsley.

4. Chill in the refrigerator or use at room temperature.

PEPPERMINT SAUCE [P]

3 handsful fresh young peppermint
leaves
2 teaspoonsful finely chopped
walnuts *or* hazelnuts
1 tablespoonful cider vinegar
Pinch of sea salt
2 teaspoonsful soured cream
(optional)

1. Place all the ingredients in a blender
container and blend until you obtain a
smooth green sauce.

2. Chill in the refrigerator if desired. This
sauce is a good accompaniment to lamb.

SOURED CREAM DRESSING [O]

½ pint (300ml) soured cream
1 small onion, finely chopped
1 tablespoonful finely chopped
dillweed *or* chervil
1 tablespoonful finely chopped basil
1 tablespoonful finely chopped
marjoram
A little brewer's yeast (optional)
Pinch of sea salt

1. Mix together all the ingredients in a
bowl.

2. Chill in the refrigerator until needed.

3. Serve with raw vegetable salads.

TOMATO RELISH [O][P]

8 large ripe continental tomatoes,
skinned
2 medium-sized onions, very finely
chopped
Pinch of sea salt
3 fl oz (90ml) dry red wine
1 teaspoonful finely chopped chilli
peppers
1 teaspoonful cayenne pepper
Handful of coarsely chopped
almonds
4 teaspoonsful cold-pressed olive oil
or sunflower oil
1 small cucumber, chopped
Few olives, stoned and chopped
Chopped parsley to serve

1. Chop the tomatoes into a non-metal
bowl. Mix together with the remaining
ingredients and chill, covered, in the
refrigerator.

2. When the relish is well-chilled, stir
again.

3. Serve sprinkled with chopped parsley.

Note: For a **protein** meal, add 1-2
tablespoonsful cider vinegar before
chilling.

VINAIGRETTE DRESSING [P]

¼ pint (140ml) cold-pressed olive oil
or sunflower oil
2½ fl oz (75ml) cider vinegar *or*
lemon juice (or more or less to taste)
Sea salt and freshly ground black
pepper to taste
1 clove garlic, crushed
Pinch of mustard powder
Chopped fresh herbs of your choice
to taste

1. Place all the ingredients in a screw-topped jar and shake to combine.

2. Chill in the refrigerator until needed. Shake again before using.

YOGURT SAUCE [P]

½ pint (300ml) natural yogurt
1 medium-sized onion, finely chopped
1 tablespoonful finely chopped dillweed
1 tablespoonful finely chopped parsley
Pinch of cayenne pepper
Sea salt to taste

1. Whisk together all the ingredients in a bowl.

2. Chill in the refrigerator until needed or serve at room temperature.

Note: This sauce, called *raita* in Indian cuisine, can also include chopped tomatoes, cucumber or coriander leaves. It is a good accompaniment to curried vegetables or meat.

HOT SAUCES

HOT CAPER SAUCE [O]

½ oz (15g) butter
1 small onion, chopped
1 tablespoonful potato flour
½ pint (300ml) Vegetable Stock
(page 37)
2 tablespoonsful finely chopped
capers
¼ pint (140ml) soured cream

1. Melt the butter in a small saucepan over low heat, add the onion and sauté until transparent.

2. Stir in the flour and cook for 1 minute. Add the vegetable stock and capers and cook gently until hot.

3. Remove from the heat and stir in the soured cream.

97

CELERIAC SAUCE Ⓞ

½ oz (15g) butter
1 tablespoonful potato flour
1 celeriac root, peeled and grated
½ pint (300ml) water
Sea salt and freshly ground black
pepper to taste
1 tablespoonful soured cream
Finely chopped celeriac leaves

1. Melt the butter in a small saucepan over low heat. Stir in the flour and cook for 1 minute. Add the celeriac and mix well.

2. Add the water, salt and pepper and cook gently until the sauce is smooth and thick. Remove from the heat.

3. Stir in the soured cream and sprinkle with celeriac leaves.

CHEESE SAUCE Ⓟ Ⓢ

1 oz (30g) butter
2 medium-sized onions, chopped
1 tablespoonful potato flour
¼ pint (140ml) single cream
¼ pint (140ml) water
7 oz (200g) Cheddar cheese, grated
1 egg yolk
4 teaspoonsful double cream
Sea salt and grated nutmeg to taste
Chopped chervil

1. Melt the butter in a medium-sized saucepan over low heat, add the onions and sauté until transparent.

2. Stir in the potato flour and cook for 1 minute. Add the single cream and water and mix well. Add the Cheddar cheese and cook, stirring, until it melts. Stir in the egg yolk and double cream and remove from the heat.

3. Season with salt and nutmeg and sprinkle with chopped chervil.

Variation:
For **starch** meals, substitute cream cheese for the Cheddar. Proceed as above.

CHIVE SAUCE Ⓞ

½ oz (15g) butter
1 tablespoonful potato flour
½ pint (300ml) Vegetable Stock
(page 37)
Generous handful of chopped chives
¼ pint (140ml) soured cream

1. Melt the butter in a small saucepan over low heat. Stir in the flour and cook for 1 minute.

2. Add the vegetable stock and cook gently until hot. Remove from the heat.

3. Stir in the chives and soured cream.

DILL SAUCE Ⓞ

½ oz (15g) butter
1 tablespoonful potato flour
½ pint (300ml) Vegetable Stock
(page 37)
Handful of finely chopped dillweed
¼ pint (140ml) soured cream

1. Melt the butter in a small saucepan over low heat. Stir in the flour and cook for 1 minute.

2. Add the vegetable stock and cook gently until the sauce has thickened.

3. Remove from the heat and mix in the dillweed and soured cream.

GARLIC SAUCE ⊙

½ oz (15g) butter
1 tablespoonful potato flour
½ pint (300ml) Vegetable Stock
(page 37)
4-6 cloves garlic, crushed
Sea salt to taste
¼ pint (140ml) soured cream

1. Melt the butter in a small saucepan over low heat. Stir in the flour and cook for 1 minute.

2. Add the vegetable stock and garlic and cook gently until the sauce has thickened. Remove from the heat, add salt if necessary and stir in the soured cream.

BLENDER P
HOLLANDAISE SAUCE

2 egg yolks
Pinch of sea salt
1 tablespoonful lemon juice
3 oz (85g) butter
Finely chopped herbs (optional)

1. Place the egg yolks, salt and lemon juice in a blender container.

2. Melt the butter in a small saucepan over low heat. Remove from the heat.

3. Blend the ingredients already in the blender for 10 seconds, then add the melted butter in a thin stream with the motor running.

4. When the sauce is thick, transfer it to a bowl or the top of a double boiler and place over hot water to keep warm.

5. Just before serving, stir in finely chopped herbs if desired.

HUNGARIAN SAUCE ⊙

1 lb (450g) tomatoes, skinned and chopped
1 oz (30g) butter
2 medium-sized onions, chopped
2 green peppers, deseeded and chopped
1 small chilli pepper, very finely chopped
Sea salt to taste
1 teaspoonful curry powder
1 teaspoonful paprika
1 tablespoonful chopped basil
1 tablespoonful chopped chervil
2 teaspoonsful soured cream

1. Purée the tomatoes in a blender or pass through a sieve. Set aside.

2. Melt the butter in a medium-sized saucepan over low heat. Add the onions, green peppers, chilli pepper, salt, curry powder and paprika and cook gently until soft.

3. Add the basil, chervil and tomatoes and just warm through. (Tomatoes should not be cooked for a **starch** meal.) Stir well, then stir in the soured cream.

ONION SAUCE O

**2 oz (55g) butter
2 Spanish onions, finely chopped
1 tablespoonful potato flour
½ pint (300ml) Vegetable Stock
(page 37) *or* water
Sea salt and white pepper to taste
¼ pint (140ml) soured cream**

1. Melt the butter in a medium-sized saucepan over low heat, add the onions and sauté until transparent. Add the flour and cook for 1 minute.

2. Pour over the vegetable stock or water, add salt and pepper to taste and cook until the sauce has thickened. Remove from the heat and purée in a blender if you prefer a smooth sauce.

3. Reheat gently and stir in the soured cream.

TOMATO SAUCE P

**1 carrot, scraped and chopped
1 stalk celery, chopped
1 celeriac root, chopped
1 small onion, chopped
2 cloves garlic, finely chopped
1 lb (450g) tomatoes, skinned and chopped
1 tablespoonful basil, finely chopped
⅓ pint (210ml) water
3 fl oz (90ml) dry white wine
Pinch of sea salt
1 teaspoonful chopped rosemary
1 teaspoonful chopped oregano**

1. Place the carrot, celery, celeriac root, onion, garlic, tomatoes, basil, water and wine in a medium-sized saucepan over moderate heat. Add a pinch of salt and cook gently, until the vegetables are very soft.

2. Remove from the heat, sprinkle with rosemary and oregano and use as is or purée in a blender.

Note: If celeriac is unavailable, substitute another root vegetable of your choice.

VEGETABLE SAUCE P

**2 onions, chopped
2 cloves garlic, chopped
1 carrot, scraped and chopped
3 ripe tomatoes, coarsely chopped
Handful of parsley, chopped
½ pint (300ml) water
1 egg
2 tablespoonsful double cream
½ tablespoonful potato flour
Sea salt to taste
Few green peppercorns
1 small chilli pepper, very finely chopped (optional)**

1. Place the onions, garlic, carrot, tomatoes, parsley and water in a medium-sized saucepan over moderate heat and cook until soft. Remove from the heat and cool slightly.

2. Place the contents of the saucepan in a blender container with the egg, cream, flour, salt, green peppercorns and chilli pepper if using and blend to a purée.

3. Reheat to serve.

Spreads and Dips

The following recipes are suitable as simple spreads for wholemeal bread and sandwiches or as dips with raw vegetables for more elegant occasions.

AVOCADO DIP

2 very ripe avocados
2 hard-boiled egg yolks
1 small onion, very finely chopped
Sea salt and freshly ground black
pepper to taste
1 oz (30g) butter, softened
Finely chopped borage and lemon
balm

1. Cut the avocados in half, remove the stones and discard.

2. Scoop out the avocado flesh into a bowl and mash until smooth with the egg yolks, onions, salt and pepper, butter and herbs.

3. This dip should be served immediately or it will discolour.

4. Serve with carrot sticks, celery sticks, cauliflower florets or raw vegetables of your choice.

Note: Vary the chopped herbs to your taste.

CHEESE DIP

6 oz (170g) fresh cream cheese
4 tablespoonsful double cream
2 tablespoonsful finely chopped
herbs
Sea salt to taste
Pinch of cayenne pepper (optional)
1 tablespoonful very finely chopped
red pepper
Tomato slices to garnish

1. Mix together all the ingredients except for the tomato slices in a bowl until well-combined.

2. Garnish with tomato slices and chill in the refrigerator if desired until needed.

CHEESE AND HERB BUTTER SPREAD

4 oz (115g) double crème cheese
(*Gervais* or *Petit-Suisse*)
4 oz (115g) butter, softened
1 medium-sized onion, very finely
chopped
Generous handful fresh chopped
herbs

1. Blend together the cheese and butter in a bowl. Mix in the onion and herbs, reserving a bit of the herbs for garnishing.

2. Sprinkle with the reserved herbs and use at room temperature or chill in the refrigerator until needed.

EGG AND ONION SPREAD

4 hard-boiled egg yolks
1 medium-sized onion, finely
chopped
Sea salt and freshly ground black
pepper to taste
Home-made Mayonnaise (page 94)
or softened butter
Onion rings and chopped chervil to
garnish

1. Mash the egg yolks in a bowl with the onion, salt, pepper and enough mayonnaise or butter to give you a spreading consistency.

2. Serve garnished with onion rings and chopped chervil.

SPICY QUARK DIP P

4 oz (115g) quark
4 tablespoonsful natural yogurt
2 tablespoonsful finely chopped
onion
1 tablespoonful chopped capers
¼ teaspoonful cayenne pepper
1 clove garlic, crushed
Sea salt to taste
Cayenne pepper, onion rings and
chopped chives to garnish

1. Sieve the quark into a bowl. Mix
together with the yogurt, onion, capers,
cayenne pepper, garlic and salt.

2. Garnish with a sprinkling of cayenne
pepper, onion rings and chives.

3. Chill in the refrigerator until needed.

Variation:
Quark Spread
Substitute softened butter for the yogurt
and add chopped green and red peppers
and herbs of your choice.

BREADS, ROLLS AND SAVOURY BAKING

Bread making is very popular among those who follow the Hay System.

Ideally, one should mill flour freshly at home, but in lieu of this, buy your flour from a reputable mill or other stockist.

Bread freezes very successfully, so you can bake in large batches if you wish. If you freeze it before it has completely cooled, it will taste fresher when it is defrosted. Slice the loaf before freezing, so that you can defrost only as many slices as you need.

Wholemeal bread can also be used to make breadcrumbs. Tear the required amount of slices into rough cubes and reduce to crumbs (in batches if necessary) in a blender.

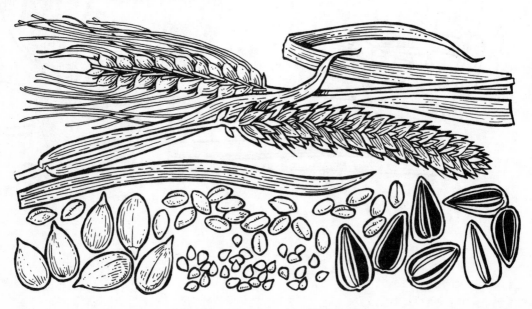

AUSTRIAN BREAKFAST ROLLS [S]

26 oz (750g) wholemeal flour
1 heaped teaspoonful sea salt
1 teaspoonful cumin seeds
1 teaspoonful aniseed
1 oz (30g) fresh yeast
2 fl oz (60ml) lukewarm water
2 teaspoonsful wholemeal flour
3 oz (85g) butter
2 tablespoonsful soured cream
Approximately ¾ pint (450ml)
lukewarm still mineral water
1 egg yolk
2 teaspoonsful water

1. Mix together the flour, salt, cumin seeds and aniseed in a large bowl.

2. Mix together the yeast, lukewarm water and wholemeal flour in a cup. Set aside until the mixture is frothy, about 15 minutes.

3. Mix the yeast mixture into the flour.

4. Melt the butter in a small saucepan. Remove from the heat and add the soured cream and lukewarm mineral water. Mix well. Add enough of this mixture to the flour to form a dough.

5. Knead the dough until it comes cleanly away from the bowl. Cover and set aside to rise in a warm place until the dough has doubled in bulk, about 45 minutes.

6. Knock the dough back, roll into a sausage shape and cut into 18 pieces. Roll each piece of dough into a ball, then press a star-shaped pattern into each ball with a biscuit cutter or the back of a knife.

7. Set aside to prove a second time.

8. Whisk the egg yolk with the water and brush the rolls with this mixture.

9. Preheat the oven to 400°F/200°C (Gas Mark 6). Bake the rolls for 20 minutes.

CUMIN STICKS [S]

10 oz (285g) wholemeal flour
2 teaspoonsful baking powder
Pinch of sea salt
1 egg yolk
5 oz (140g) butter
Soured cream
1 egg yolk, whisked with a little water
Sea salt and cumin seeds to sprinkle

1. Mix together the flour, baking powder and salt in a bowl. Mix in the egg yolk. Cut in the butter until the mixture resembles breadcrumbs, then add enough soured cream, spoonful by spoonful to make a dough that holds together.

2. Knead the dough thoroughly but quickly to avoid making it too warm.

3. Turn the dough out onto a lightly floured pastry board and roll out to a thickness of approximately ½ inch (1.25cm). With a sharp knife, cut into sticks or straws.

4. Preheat the oven to 375°F/190°C (Gas Mark 5).

5. Brush the sticks with the egg yolk mixture, sprinkle with salt and cumin seeds.

6. Place the cumin sticks on a baking sheet and bake until golden, taking care that the sticks do not overbrown.

ONION BREAD [S]

1 lb (450g) freshly milled wholemeal
flour
4 teaspoonsful sea salt
1½ oz (40g) fresh yeast
2 fl oz (60ml) lukewarm water
8 fl oz (240ml) still mineral water
4 teaspoonsful soured cream
4 teaspoonsful corn oil
2 egg yolks
7 oz (200g) onions, chopped
Butter to grease
Wholemeal flour to dust

1. Place the flour and salt in a medium-
sized bowl.

2. Cream the yeast with the lukewarm
water and set aside until it is frothy,
about 15 minutes.

3. Warm the mineral water and mix with
the soured cream. Add the yeast mixture
to the flour, then incorporate the mineral
water mixture, corn oil and egg yolks,
working all the ingredients into a firm
dough. Work the onions into the dough,
cover the dough and set aside in a warm
place to allow it to rise until it has
doubled in bulk. Form into a loaf and
set aside to prove again.

4. Preheat the oven to 400°F/180°C (Gas
Mark 6).

5. Place the onion loaf on a greased and
floured baking sheet. Place a tin of water
in the bottom of the oven and bake the
bread for about 1 hour, until it is golden-
brown and sounds hollow when it is
lightly tapped.

ONION FLAN [S]

Pastry:
½ lb (225g) wholemeal flour
Pinch of sea salt
Pinch of baking powder
4 oz (115g) butter
1-1½ tablespoonsful still mineral
water
1 egg yolk

Filling:
1 oz (30g) butter
1 lb (450g) onions, chopped
½ pint (300ml) soured cream
2 egg yolks
Pinch of nutmeg
Sea salt and freshly ground black
pepper to taste
Butter to grease
Wholemeal flour to dust

1. Mix together the flour, salt and
baking powder in a bowl. Cut in the
butter until the mixture resembles
breadcrumbs. Whisk together the mineral
water and egg yolk in a cup. Add to the
flour mixture and combine well. Roll the
pastry into a ball, cover with cling film
and chill in the refrigerator for 30
minutes.

2. Meanwhile, make the filling. Melt the
butter in a medium-sized saucepan over
low heat and sauté the onions until
transparent. Set aside to cool.

3. Mix the onions with the soured
cream. Whisk the egg yolks and add to
the filling along with the nutmeg, and
salt and pepper.

4. Grease a flan tin and dust with flour.

5. Roll out the pastry thinly to fit the
tin, pick up with the rolling pin and
place in the tin. Trim if necessary and
flute the edges.

6. Preheat the oven to 350°F/180°C (Gas Mark 4).

7. Fill the pastry shell with the onion mixture. Bake for about 30 minutes, until the pastry and filling are golden.

PIZZA S

Dough:
1 oz (30g) fresh yeast
2 fl oz (60ml) lukewarm water
10 oz (285g) wholemeal flour
2 oz (55g) butter
Pinch of sea salt
½ teaspoonful ground coriander seeds
½ teaspoonful ground cumin seeds
Iced water

Filling:
1 oz (30g) butter
10 oz (285g) onions, chopped
1 green pepper, deseeded and chopped
1 red pepper, deseeded and chopped
1 yellow pepper, deseeded and chopped
1 teaspoonful chopped basil
1 teaspoonful chopped chervil
½ teaspoonful chopped thyme
½ teaspoonful chopped oregano
4 oz (115g) cream cheese
4 tomatoes, skinned and sliced

1. First make the dough base. Cream the yeast with the water and set aside until frothy, about 15 minutes.

2. Tip the flour into a bowl. Make a well in the centre and pour in the yeast mixture. Mix well. Add most of the butter, salt, coriander and cumin and mix again. Add just enough iced water, spoonful by spoonful, then drop by drop to make a firm but pliable dough. Knead it thoroughly, cover and set aside in a warm place and allow to rise until the dough has doubled in bulk.

3. Grease a large flan tin with the remaining butter. Roll the dough out to 2 inches larger in diameter than the tin, pick it up with the rolling pin and place in the tin. Trim if necessary. Allow to rest while preparing the filling.

4. Preheat the oven to 350°F/180°C (Gas Mark 4).

5. Make the filling. Melt the butter in a large saucepan over low heat, add the onions and peppers and cook gently until soft. Add the basil, chervil, thyme and oregano and mix well. Spread on the pizza base and spread spoonfuls of cream cheese over this. Bake for 30 minutes, until golden-brown.

6. When the pizza is baked, top it with sliced tomatoes and return to the oven. Turn the oven off so that the tomatoes warm, but don't cook. Serve immediately.

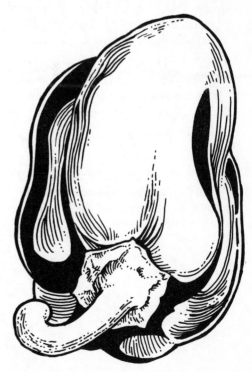

SESAME SEED BISCUITS [S]

8 oz (225g) wholemeal flour
½ teaspoonful salt
7 oz (200g) butter
1-1½ tablespoonsful iced water
2 oz (55g) sesame seeds, toasted

1. Mix together the flour and salt in a bowl. Cut in 6 oz (170g) of the butter until the mixture resembles breadcrumbs. Add the water a few drops at a time, mixing after each addition. Add only enough water to make a dough that will hold together. Form the dough into a ball.

2. Turn the dough out onto a lightly floured pastry board and roll out to a thickness of ½ inch (1.25cm). Soften the remaining butter and spread on the dough. Fold into thirds like a letter and press down slightly. Chill in the refrigerator for at least 30 minutes.

3. Roll the chilled dough out again to a thickness of ½ inch (1.25cm). Sprinkle with the sesame seeds, pressing them lightly into the dough.

4. Preheat the oven to 350°F/180°C (Gas Mark 4).

5. Cut the dough into rounds with a 2-inch (5cm) biscuit cutter. Place the rounds on an ungreased sheet and bake for 15-20 minutes, until golden.

SOURED CREAM SCONES [S]

½ lb (225g) wholemeal flour
1 tablespoonful baking powder
½ teaspoonful sea salt
2 oz (55g) butter
2 egg yolks
4 fl oz (120ml) soured cream

1. Mix together the flour, baking powder and salt in a bowl. Cut in the butter until the mixture resembles breadcrumbs. Make a well in the centre.

2. Whisk the egg yolks slightly in a cup, then combine with the soured cream. Pour this mixture into the well and stir with a fork to moisten all the ingredients. Avoid overmixing.

3. Turn the mixture out onto a floured pastry board and knead lightly 5 or 6 times. Roll out to a thickness of ½ inch (1.25cm). Cut into rounds with a 2-inch (5cm) biscuit cutter.

4. Place a frying pan over moderate heat. When it is hot, bake the scones for about 10 minutes on each side.

WHOLEMEAL BAPS [S]

2¼ lb (1kg) wholemeal flour
3 oz (85g) butter, melted
2 oz (55g) fresh yeast
1 oz (25g) sea salt
1 teaspoonful aniseed
1 teaspoonful fennel seeds
1 pint (600ml) still mineral water
4 teaspoonsful soured cream
Sesame *or* poppy seeds
Butter to grease
Wholemeal flour to dust

1. Mix together all the ingredients except the sesame or poppy seeds in a bowl and combine into a dough, adding a little more mineral water if the dough is too stiff. Knead well, cover and set aside in a warm place to allow the dough to rise until it has doubled in bulk.

2. Form the dough into baps, sprinkle with water and sesame or poppy seeds and set aside to prove again on a greased and floured baking sheet.

3. Preheat the oven to 400°F/200°C (Gas Mark 6). Bake the baps for about 30 minutes, depending on size, until they are golden-brown.

WHOLEMEAL BREAD [S]

If you are baking bread for the first time, buy the sourdough starter from a baker or health food shop. After that, you can make your own starter at home. Excellent seasonings for bread are cumin, coriander, fennel, anise and sesame seeds, which you can toast lightly before adding them to the dough. Sunflower or pumpkin seeds may also be added.

The best liquid to use in bread making is whey, but if this is not available, use buttermilk diluted with water in the proportions given in the recipes. A moister loaf can be made with rye flour alone. The following recipe makes 5 or 6 loaves of bread.

3 lb (1.5kg) wholemeal flour
2¼ lb (1kg) rye flour
Seasonings and salt to taste (see above)
10 oz (285g) sourdough starter
1 oz (30g) yeast
2 fl oz (60ml) lukewarm water
1 pint (600ml) buttermilk
3 pints (1.75 litres) warm water

1. Mix together the wholemeal flour and rye flour in a very large bowl, adding seasonings and salt to taste.

2. Add the sourdough starter.

3. Mix the yeast with the lukewarm water and set aside until the mixture is frothy, about 15 minutes. Add to the flours and starter.

4. Mix together the buttermilk and warm water, add to the flour and mix to make a dough. Knead well until the dough is no longer sticky, then dust with flour and set aside in a warm place until it has almost doubled in bulk (45 minutes to 1 hour).

5. Knock back the dough and knead again. Break off about 10 oz (285g) of the dough and store in a screw-topped jar in the refrigerator ready for the next time you are going to bake. This will be the new starter.

6. Form the remaining dough into 5 or 6 cottage loaves or divide it between loaf tins and set aside to prove a second time.

7. Preheat the oven to 400°F/200°C (Gas Mark 6).

8. Bake the bread (in batches if necessary), reducing the oven heat after 15 minutes to 350°F/180°F (Gas Mark 4). Continue to bake for a total of 1 hour until it is well-risen and golden-brown.

9. Test for doneness by tapping the bread lightly. If it sounds hollow, return to the oven and turn off the heat. Place in a tin of water in the bottom of the oven and allow the bread to cool slightly. The steam from the water will prevent the crust from becoming too hard. (You can also sprinkle the bread with water before it has finished baking.

WHOLEMEAL ROLLS [S]

2¼ lb (1kg) wholemeal flour
2 teaspoonsful ground coriander,
fennel or anise seeds
1 oz (30g) salt
5 oz (140g) bran or oatflakes
(optional)
1¼ pints (750ml) whey, still mineral
water or ½ pint (300ml) buttermilk
diluted with ¾ pint (450ml) warm
water
1½ oz (40g) fresh yeast
Poppy or sesame seeds to sprinkle

1. Place the flour in a large bowl and
mix in the coriander, fennel or anise
seeds and salt. Stir in the bran or
oakflakes if using.

2. If you can obtain whey, warm it
slightly and cream in the yeast. If not,
warm the mineral water or diluted
buttermilk and cream in the yeast. Make
a well in the centre of the flour and pour
in the yeast mixture. Set aside until
frothy, about 15 minutes.

3. Work the yeast mixture into the flour
to make a dough, then knead until
smooth, either with an electric mixer
fitted with a dough hook or by hand.
Cover and leave in a warm place to rise
until it has doubled in bulk, about 45
minutes.

4. Divide into 20-30 rolls (whatever
shape you like), place on floured baking
sheets and sprinkle with water. Sprinkle
with poppy or sesame seeds and set aside
to prove once more.

5. Preheat the oven to 400°F/200°C (Gas
Mark 6).

6. Stand a tin of water in the bottom of
the oven to prevent the crust from
getting too hard. Bake the rolls for about
30 minutes until golden-brown.

WHOLEWHEAT SALT [S]
STICKS

1 oz (30g) fresh yeast
½ pint (300ml) lukewarm water
1 lb (450g) freshly milled wholemeal
flour
1 teaspoonful salt
Coarse sea salt to sprinkle

1. Cream the yeast with the lukewarm
water. Set aside until the mixture is
frothy, about 15 minutes.

2. Place the flour in a medium-sized
bowl and add the yeast mixture and salt.
Form into a dough and knead well.
Cover and allow to rise for 15 minutes.

3. Knead the dough again, then divide
into 8 pieces and roll out into squares.
Cut each square diagonally in half to
make 16 triangles.

4. With your right hand, roll one of the
straight sides towards the opposite point;
pull the point out a bit with your left
hand and secure it around the roll.
Brush with water and sprinkle liberally
with coarse salt. Allow to rise again.

5. Preheat the oven to 375°F/190°C (Gas
Mark 5).

6. Place the rolls on a baking sheet and
bake for about 15 minutes.

SWEETS

The Hay System is not difficult to follow, even when one is dining out, with one exception — dessert, which usually contains all sorts of 'forbidden fruits', particularly refined carbohydrates such as white sugar, white flour and all the foods prepared with them.

When you are cooking at home, however, you can indulge in cakes, pies and other sweets if you adapt your recipes to include wholemeal flour (for starch meals) and substitute honey or fructose (fruit sugar) for white sugar when sweetening puddings, ice creams and fruits. Remember that fructose and honey are much sweeter than ordinary sugar, so cut down the amount you normally use.

The following recipes have been adapted to provide you with a starting point, which will allow you to create many wonderful desserts that are in keeping with the Hay System.

BANANA CREAM TART S

Pastry shell:
½ lb (225g) wholemeal flour
1 teaspoonful baking powder
2 egg yolks
Pinch of sea salt
2 oz (55g) fructose (fruit sugar)
3 oz (85g) cold butter, diced
Butter to grease

Banana Cream Filling:
1 tablespoonful fructose (fruit sugar)
Pinch of sea salt
3 tablespoonsful wholemeal flour
12 fl oz (360ml) single cream
1 egg yolk
¼ teaspoonful vanilla essence
(optional)
4 ripe bananas

1. Mix together the flour and baking powder and sift into a bowl. Make a well in the centre.

2. Place the egg yolks, salt, fructose and butter into the well and mix with your hands to form a smooth dough. Roll into a ball, wrap in cling film and set aside in the refrigerator to rest for at least 30 minutes.

3. Grease a 9-inch (22.5cm) flan dish. Preheat the oven to 400°F/200°C (Gas Mark 6).

4. Roll out the pastry and use to line the prepared dish. Crumple a sheet of aluminium foil, fill with beans or rice and bake 'blind' for 15-20 minutes. Remove from the oven and cool.

5. Make the filling. Mix together the fructose, salt and flour in a medium-sized saucepan. Add the cream gradually. Place over low heat and cook, stirring constantly until the mixture has thickened. Continue to cook for a further 3 minutes. Remove from the heat and stir some of the cream mixture into the egg yolk, then return to the pan and cook 1 minute further. Remove from the heat and stir in the vanilla essence if using. Cool thoroughly.

6. When both the pastry shell and filling are cool, slice the bananas into the pastry shell, covering the base. Spoon the cream mixture over. Chill in the refrigerator until quite cold.

CARROT NUT PUDDING Ⓢ

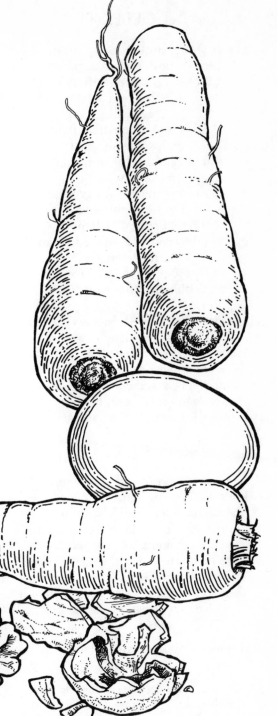

10 oz (285g) carrots, scraped and
coarsely grated
10 oz (285g) walnuts, coarsely grated
5 oz (140g) fructose (fruit sugar) *or*
honey
1 egg yolk
2 tablespoonsful double cream
1 tablespoonful baking powder
Butter to grease
Whipped cream to serve

1. Mix together the carrots, walnuts,
fructose, egg yolk, cream and baking
powder in a bowl.

2. Turn the mixture into a greased cake
tin and place in a cold oven.

3. Turn the oven on to 350°F/180°C
(Gas Mark 4). Bake the cake for 50
minutes, or until a wooden cocktail stick
inserted in the centre comes out clean.

4. Serve with whipped cream.

KUGELHOPF S

5 oz (140g) stoned dates, chopped
¼ pint (140ml) still mineral wtaer
3 oz (85g) butter, softened
Pinch of sea salt
2 egg yolks
1 lb (450g) wholemeal flour
1 oz (30g) fresh yeast
8 fl oz (240ml) lukewarm still
mineral water
2 oz (55g) hazelnuts, ground
3 oz (85g) sultanas
Grated rind of 1 lemon
1½ tablespoonful soured cream
Butter to grease
1 oz (30g) hazelnuts, ground
Wholemeal flour to dust

1. Place the chopped dates and ¼ pint (140ml) mineral water in a small saucepan over moderate heat and cook for a few minutes to soften, then remove from the heat and purée in a blender. Set aside to cool. Cream the date purée with the softened butter, salt and egg yolks.

2. Place the flour in a bowl.

3. Cream the yeast with 2 tablespoonful of the remaining mineral water and set the mixture aside until it is frothy, about 15 minutes, then add to the flour along with the hazelnuts, sultanas, lemon rind, date purée, the rest of the mineral water and the soured cream. Knead the dough, then set aside in a warm place to allow it to rise until it has doubled in bulk, about 1 hour.

4. Preheat the oven to 400°F/200°C (Gas Mark 6).

5. Grease a kugelhopf mould, sprinkle with ground hazelnuts and dust with flour. Place the dough in the mould, cover and set aside to prove for a further 30 minutes.

6. Bake for about 45 minutes, until a wooden cocktail stick inserted in the centre comes out clean.

NUT BAKE S

1 pint (600ml) water
Handful of sultanas
10 oz (285g) wheat or barley flakes
Butter to grease
1½ tablespoonful soured cream
1½ tablespoonful fructose
4 oz (115g) butter
4 oz (115g) walnuts, ground
½ teaspoonful ground cinnamon
1 teaspoonful grated lemon rind

1. Pour the water into a medium-sized saucepan, add a pinch of salt and the sultanas and bring to the boil. Tip in the wheat or barley flakes, remove from the heat, cover the pan and set aside to allow the grain to swell and absorb the water.

2. Preheat the oven to 350°F/180°C (Gas Mark 4). Grease an ovenproof dish.

3. When all the water has been absorbed by the grain, stir in the fructose, butter, ground nuts, cinnamon and lemon rind and turn the mixture into the prepared dish. Bake until golden brown, 20-30 minutes.

SULTANA SLICES $\boxed{\text{S}}$

1 lb (450g) wholemeal flour
1 oz (30g) fresh yeast
2 tablespoonsful honey
¼ pint (140ml) lukewarm still
mineral water
1½ tablespoonsful fructose
2½ tablespoonsful soured cream
2 egg yolks
2½ oz (70g) butter, softened
Pinch of sea salt
1 teaspoonful lemon rind*
¾ lb (340g) sultanas
Fructose (fruit sugar) to sprinkle
1 teaspoonful ground cinnamon
Butter to grease
Wholemeal flour to dust

1. Sift the flour into a medium-sized bowl to remove the bran. Make a well in the centre.

2. Cream the yeast with the mineral water to which you have added the honey. Set aside until the mixture is frothy, about 15 minutes.

3. Pour the yeast mixture into the well. Add the soured cream, egg yolks, butter, salt and lemon rind and mix to form a dough. Cover the dough and set aside in a warm place to allow it to rise until it is doubled in bulk, about 45 minutes.

4. Roll the dough out to a thickness of about ½-inch (1.25cm). Sprinkle with the sultanas, fructose and cinnamon. Roll up and with a sharp knife, cut into slices about 1 inch (2.5cm) wide. Grease and flour a baking sheet, place the sultana slices on it and allow to prove a second time.

5. Preheat the oven to 350°F/180°C (Gas Mark 4). Bake for about 25 minutes, until golden.

*From lemon guaranteed unsprayed with fungicide.

APPLE SNOW $\boxed{\text{P}}$

4 egg whites
Pinch of sea salt
2 tablespoonsful honey
1 recipe quantity Apple Sauce
(page 94)
Ground cinnamon to sprinkle

1. Place the egg whites and salt in a deep bowl, preferably a copper one. Whisk with a wire wisk until foamy, then add the honey and whisk until stiff peaks form.

2. Place the apple sauce in another bowl. Stir in a spoonful of the egg whites to lighten the mixture, then gently fold in the remaining egg whites, using a figure-of-eight motion.

3. To serve, turn into a serving bowl, sprinkle with cinnamon and serve at room temperature, or chill in the refrigerator. Alternatively, the mixture can be frozen in ice cube trays and served as an ice.

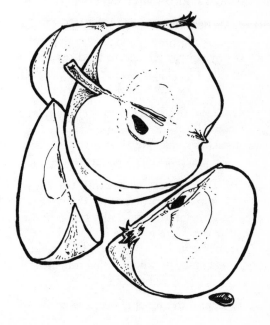

BAKED APPLE PUDDING [P]

¾ pint (425ml) water
Juice of ½ lemon
4 large tart cooking apples
3 oz (85g) honey
Butter to grease
4 oz (115g) unsalted butter, softened
3 oz (85g) honey
3 eggs, separated
2 oz (55g) almonds, ground
1 tablespoonful lemon juice
Pinch of sea salt

1. Pour the water into a medium-sized saucepan and stir in the lemon juice.

2. Core the apples, cut in half crossways and drop into the acidulated water. Stir in the honey. Place over moderate heat and bring to the boil, stirring occasionally, reduce the heat and simmer for 8-10 minutes, until the apples are tender. Remove the apples from the pan with a slotted spoon and leave to drain.

3. Preheat the oven to 350°F/180°C (Gas Mark 4). Grease a shallow ovenproof dish just large enough to hold the apples in one layer. Place the apples in the dish, cut side down.

4. Cream the butter with the honey in a bowl. Whisk in the egg yolks one at a time, then add the almonds and lemon juice and mix well. Set aside.

5. Whisk the egg whites with the salt in a deep bowl, preferably a copper one, until they form stiff peaks. Stir a bit of the egg white mixture into the butter mixture to lighten it, then fold in the remaining egg whites, using a figure-of-eight motion.

6. Spread the topping over the apples in the dish and bake for about 30 minutes, until golden.

7. Serve slightly warm or at room temperature.

BANANA PARFAIT [S]

½ pint (300ml) soured cream
1 tablespoonful honey
2 ripe bananas, mashed
2 oz (55g) walnuts, finely chopped

1. Place the soured cream in a bowl. Add the honey and mashed bananas and mix well.

2. Layer the banana mixture in four dessert glasses with the walnuts, reserving a bit of the walnuts to sprinkle on top. Chill in the refrigerator until quite cold.

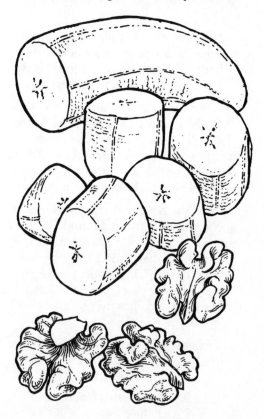

FROZEN RASPBERRY YOGURT [P]

**½ lb (225g) fresh raspberries
3 oz (85g) honey
16 fl oz (480ml) natural yogurt**

1. Purée the raspberries with the honey in a blender.

2. Place the yogurt in a bowl. Add the raspberry purée and mix well.

3. Place the mixture into an ice cream machine and follow the manufacturer's directions for freezing. Alternatively, pour into an ice cube tray and place in the freezer until half-frozen. Tip into a bowl and whisk well, then return to the freezer for 1-2 hours.

Variations:
Substitute any of the allowed fruits for the raspberries and adjust the amount of honey to suit the sweetness of the fruit. Proceed as above.

VANILLA ICE CREAM [O]

**2 egg yolks
1½ tablespoonsful fructose
½ teaspoonful vanilla essence
½ pint (300ml) double cream, whipped**

1. Whisk together the egg yolks, fructose and vanilla essence.

2. Fold the egg mixture into the whipped cream. Pour into an ice cube tray or shallow tin and freeze for at least 2 hours.

Variation:
Hazelnut Ice Cream
Add 2 oz (55g) finely ground hazelnuts and 1 tablespoonful rum to the egg mixture before folding into the cream. Proceed as above.

DRINKS

It is best not to drink at all during a meal, but for those who find this difficult, the following advice should be taken into consideration.

HOT DRINKS

TEA
Avoid drinking Indian or Chinese tea. Choose instead from the many herbal teas available. Unless you have been advised by your doctor to drink a particular tea for medicinal reasons, experiment with all the different herbal teas that take your fancy and keep a variety to hand. All teas should be taken without sugar.

COFFEE
Weak fresh coffee may be taken in conjunction with either starch or protein meals. Coffee substitutes should not be used with protein meals.

COLD DRINKS

HERBAL TEAS
Cold herbal teas, sweetened with honey, make a very refreshing summer drink.

FRESHLY PRESSED FRUIT JUICE
Fresh fruit juice is very healthy, as well as thirst-quenching. Pressing your own juice is a good way of using up fallings in the summer and autumn months. Acid fruit juices should not be served with a starch meal.

VEGETABLE JUICE
Almost any vegetable can be turned into juice. Beetroot and carrot juice are already popular, but you can create vegetable cocktails by mixing either of these with tomato juice, spinach juice or cucumber juice, adding a few herb leaves.

Do not only drink the juice of fruits and vegetables. The fibre in fruits and vegetables is necessary to the body; this is lost in juice extraction.

MILK DRINKS
If you can buy unpasteurized milk, do so. Buttermilk is neutral, but all other types of milk are incompatible with starch meals.

You can make delicious milk shakes by adding bananas, berries or other fruits to milk in a blender. Another thirst-quenching 'shake' can be made by combining yogurt and fruit juice. Milk should not be drunk with a meat meal. Look upon milk as a food, not a drink, and take in moderation only.

ALCOHOLIC DRINKS

Alcoholic drinks should be taken in moderation. Avoid sweet wines, sherries, liqueurs and sugary cocktails. A good dry wine, however, is compatible with protein meals and helps the digestion. Beer should be avoided at or near a protein meal since it is classed as a carbohydrate. Cider should not be drunk with a starch meal, due to its apple base.

If you have medical problems such as gout or rheumatism, you should avoid alcohol completely. If you have other problems, your doctor can help to advise you.

TABLE OF COMPATIBLE FOODS

Reproduced from *Food Combining For Health* (Thorsons, 1984)
by kind permission of the authors, Doris Grant and Jean Joice.

Columms I and III are incompatible

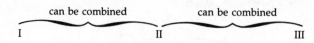

I	II	III
For Protein meals	**Neutral Foods** can be combined with either Col. I or Col. III.	**For Starch meals**

PROTEINS	**NUTS**	**CEREALS**
Meat of all kinds: Beef, lamb, pork, venison	All except peanuts	Wholegrain: Wheat, barley, maize, oats, millet, rice (brown, unpolished), rye
Poultry: Chicken, duck, goose, turkey	**FATS**	Bread 100% wholewheat
Game: Pheasant, partridge, grouse, hare	Butter Cream Egg yolks	Flour 100% or 85% Oatmeal — medium
Fish of all kinds including shellfish	Olive oil (virgin) Sunflower seed oil Sesame seed oil (cold pressed)	
Eggs Cheese Milk (combines best with fruit and should not be served at a meat meal) Yogurt		

FRUITS	**VEGETABLES**	**SWEET FRUITS**
Apples	All green and root vegetables except potatoes and Jerusalem artichokes	Bananas – ripe
Apricots (fresh & dried)	Asparagus	Dates
Blackberries	Aubergines	Figs (fresh & dried)
Blueberries	Beans (all fresh green beans)	Grapes – extra sweet
Cherries	Beetroot	Papaya if *very* ripe
Currants (black, red or white if ripe)	Broccoli	Pears if *very* sweet and ripe
Gooseberries (if ripe)	Brussels sprouts	Currants
Grapefruit	Cabbage	Raisins
Grapes	Calabrese	Sultanas
Kiwis	Carrots	
Lemons	Cauliflower	**VEGETABLES**
Limes	Celery	
Loganberries	Celeriac	Potatoes
Mangoes	Courgettes (zucchini)	Jerusalem artichokes
Melons (best eaten *alone* as a fruit meal)	Kohlrabi	
Nectarines	Leeks	**MILK & YOGURT**
Oranges	Marrow (squash)	
Papayas	Mushrooms	only in moderation
Pears	Onions	
Pineapples	Parsnips	
Prunes (for occasional use)	Peas	
Raspberries	Spinach	
Satsumas	Swedes (rutabagas)	
Strawberries	Turnips	
Tangerines		

N.B. plums and cranberries
are *not* recommended

Columms I and III are incompatible

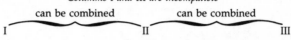

can be combined   can be combined

I   II   III

For Protein meals	**Neutral Foods** can be combined with either Col. I or Col. III.	**For Starch meals**
SALAD DRESSINGS	SALADINGS	SALAD DRESSINGS
French dressing made with oil and lemon juice or apple cider vinegar Cream dressing Mayonnaise (homemade)	Avocados Chicory Corn salad Cucumber Endive Fennel Garlic Lettuce Mustard & cress Peppers, red and green Radishes Spring onions Sprouted legumes Sprouted seeds Tomatoes (uncooked) Watercress	Sweet or soured cream Olive oil or cold pressed seed oils Fresh tomato juice with oil and seasoning
	HERBS & FLAVOURINGS	
	Chives Mint Parsley Sage Tarragon Thyme Grated lemon rind Grated orange rind	
	SEEDS	
	Sunflower Sesame Pumpkin	
	BRAN	
	Wheat or oat bran Wheatgerm	
SUGAR SUBSTITUTE	SUGAR SUBSTITUTE	SUGARS
Diluted frozen orange juice	Raisins and raisin juice Honey Maple syrup	Barbados sugar Honey – in strict moderation
FOR VEGETARIANS (but not recommended)		
Legumes Lentils Soya beans Kidney beans Chick peas Butter beans Pinto beans		
ALCOHOL	ALCOHOL	ALCOHOL
Dry red and white wines Dry cider	Whisky Gin	Ale Beer

INDEX

FOOD COMBINING FOR HEALTH
Doris Grant and Jean Joice

There is only one cause of all disease — wrong chemical conditions in the body — and incorrect nutrition contributes towards these conditions. Doris Grant and Jean Joice here take a fresh look at a successful nutritional system *which removes the obstacles modern diet places upon nature's own healing powers.* Based upon a system devised by Dr. William Howard Hay in 1908 it argues that since the body uses acids to digest proteins and alkalis to digest starches, mixing the two in one meal will lead not only to sluggish digestion, but also, inevitably, to more serious chronic conditions such as ulcers, allergies and obesity. *No claims to cures are made other than of allowing the body to heal itself.* Contains many testimonials of sufferers from degenerative disease who have arrested, or reversed, the course of their illness by this method.

FOOD COMBINING FOR VEGETARIANS
Jackie Le Tissier

Since the bestselling *Food Combining for Health* launched a dieting revolution, Dr Hay's diet has improved the health and eating habits of thousands. Now the Hay system has been adapted especially for *vegetarians*.

Discover:
- Delicious recipes for every occasion
- Which foods to eat and which to avoid
- Original menus and serving suggestions and *much much more!*

What *is* food combining! A wonderful way of eating for health which can be adopted for life. Simply by separating starch from protein and increasing the quantity of alkaline foods in your daily diet you can work *with* your body to:

- Lose weight without worry
- Increase your health and vitality
- Improve your resistance to illness.

Jackie Le Tissier has been vegetarian food combining for years. Her inspiring recipes will show you how to put the Hay Diet into practice.